EXCURSIONS IN THE
REAL WORLD

BY THE SAME AUTHOR

WILLIAM TREVOR

Excursions in the Real World

WITH ILLUSTRATIONS
BY
LUCY WILLIS

Alfred A. Knopf Canada

PUBLISHED BY ALFRED A. KNOPF CANADA

Copyright © 1993 by William Trevor
Copyright © 1993 in the illustrations by Lucy Willis

All rights reserved under International
and Pan-American Copyright Conventions.
Published in Canada in 1993 by Alfred A. Knopf
Canada, Toronto, and simultaneously in Great Britain by
Hutchinson, Random Century Group Limited.
Distributed by Random House of Canada Limited, Toronto

Canadian Cataloguing in Publication Data
Trevor, William, 1928–
Excursions in the real world

ISBN 0–394–28000–8

1. Trevor, William, 1928–   . 2. Authors,
English – 20th century – Biography. I. Title.

PR6070.R4Z465   1993   823'.914   C93–094030–X

First Canadian Edition

Phototypeset by Falcon Graphic Art Ltd.
Printed by Mackays of Chatham PLC, Chatham, Kent

Toronto, New York, London, Sydney, Auckland

FOR MY BROTHER AND SISTER

ACKNOWLEDGEMENTS

Sometimes in a different form, a number of these essays first appeared in: *Antaeus, Bad Trips* (edited by Keath Fraser, Vintage Books), the *Daily Telegraph*, the *Guardian*, the *Hudson Review*, the *Irish Times*, the *London Magazine*, the *New Statesman*, the *New Yorker*, *Nova*, the *Observer*, the *Oldie, Places* (edited by Ronald Blythe, Oxford University Press), the *Spectator*. Acknowledgements are also made to the Lemon Tree Press and Virago.

CONTENTS

INTRODUCTION

THE SKETCHES HERE are of real people, almost all of whom are no longer alive. Some briefly encountered, others well known over many years, a few not met at all, these are people who for one reason or another have remained snagged in the memory. There have been others, of course, but naturally you have to draw the line.

Places do not die as people do, but they often change so fundamentally that little is left of what once they were. The landscape of the Nire Valley that spreads over a northern part of County Waterford is timeless, but the Dublin remembered here is the Dublin of several pasts, and elsewhere among these impressions there is that same dichotomy.

In any record of personal fascinations and enthusiasms, the recorder cannot remain entirely in the shadows, much as he might wish to do so. In the spring of 1992 the *Guardian* published a weekly series in which novelists from different countries wrote about who they were — or how they saw themselves — in terms of their nationality. The following extract from what I myself contributed may serve as an introduction to the figure whose memory has been tapped in order to provide these forays from the territory of fiction into that of reality as it was.

★

Being Irish is complicated, in my case, by the fact that I am a writer of fiction. One circumstance influences the other: nationality seems irrelevant in the loose, uncharted world of art, then suddenly raises its voice; fiction insists on universality, then equally insists that a degree of parochialism can often best achieve this. A muddle of contradiction prevails, but since the practice of any art has to do with establishing order, muddles should be grist to the artistic mill. Or so at least you can pretend.

Writing is a professional activity, yet when fiction is the end product it must necessarily also be a personal one. As you engage in it, you cannot escape the person you are, even if you are not inquisitive about yourself and even though you instinctively know that the less your fingerprints

blur your novels and stories the better. All fiction has its autobiographical roots in the sense that as a person you are your characters' litmus
paper, their single link with reality. They taste as you taste, they hear
as you hear. The blue they see is your blue, the pain they experience is
your pain, their physical pleasure is what you know yourself. And the
workings of memory you cull from yourself also.

> His first memory was of a black iron gate, of his own hands upon
> it, and of his uncle driving through the gateway in a model–T Ford.
> These images, and that of his uncle's bespectacled face perspiring, were
> all in sunshine . . . He remembered also, at some later time, eating
> tinned tomato soup in a house that was not the house of his aunt and
> uncle; he remembered a tap near a greenhouse; he remembered eating
> an ice-cream outside Horgan's Picture House while his aunt engaged
> another woman in conversation.

They are my memories too, but I am not the character in the
story. The projection is a natural one because the town, and the
incidents described, are to hand, and the period coincides. There's
no point in rejecting reality just for the sake of it.

This bringing together of the person and the writer is an element
in the professional's craft. A more fundamental one, and more difficult,
is prising them apart in the first place. Born Irish, I observe the world
through Irish sensibilities, take for granted an Irish way of doing things,
am marked by small idiosyncrasies of behaviour and accent, and am
reminded of familiarities of early environment when I'm separated from
them. The bee-loud glade and the linnet's wings of Yeats's lament, the
Mountains of Mourne sweeping down to the sea, are sweet nourishment
for the exile. Sweeter still the aeroplane touching down at Dublin or
Cork, the car crawling on to the quays at Rosslare. When the green
jerseys swarm on to the pitch I will them passionately on. When an
atrocity is an Irish one I am ashamed.

The writer's stance is different. He needs space and cool; sentiment
is suspect. Awkward questions, posed to himself, are his stock-in-trade.
He attempts to extract an essence from the truth by turning it into what
John Updike has called 'fiction's shapely lies'. To do so, he has to stand
back — so far that he finds himself beyond the pale, outside the society
he comments upon in order to get a better view of it. Time, simply by

passing, does not supply that distance: in my case, what was absorbed during my provincial childhood has long since germinated into raw material, but it is valueless in itself.

I was fortunate that my accident of birth actually placed me on the edge of things. I was born into a minority that all my life has seemed in danger of withering away. This was smalltime Protestant stock, far removed from the well-to-do Ascendancy of the recent past yet without much of a place in de Valera's new Catholic Ireland. The insult and repression that for centuries had been the response to Irish aspirations, the murders perpetrated by the Black and Tans, the heartbreak of the Civil War, were all to be expunged in de Valera's dream of a land 'bright with cosy homesteads, whose fields and villages would be joyous with the sounds of industry, with the romping of sturdy children, the contests of athletic youths, the laughter of comely maidens; whose firesides would be forums for the wisdom of old age'.

But dreams remain dreams unless practical steps are taken: some body of good men would have to ensure that all the people of Ireland lived the life 'that God desires men should live'. Quite naturally, de Valera turned to his priests, and quite naturally Protestants felt uneasy.

On my father's side the family had been Catholic until late in the eighteenth century, when they turned in order to survive the Penal Laws. The gesture was hardly worth the effort: their sparse acres of land in County Roscommon were among the worst in Ireland and the farmhouse that accompanied them — built without foundations — was in perpetual danger of collapse, which finally it succumbed to. Bankruptcy finished matters off. On my mother's side there was sturdy Ulster Protestantism for as long as anyone could remember, and a similar small-farming background, near Loughgall in Co. Armagh.

In the seaside town of Youghal, where my father was a bank clerk in the early nineteen thirties, the last flickers of the old order were still evident, while the terrible beauty of 1916 spawned stern Christian Brothers, the new-style Irish language, and school history books that were as biased in their definitions as the old King-and-Empire ones had been in theirs. Among the Protestants of the town and the neighbourhood the class barriers had fallen in the interests of unity. The remnants of the Big House families, those who had chosen not to run away, opened their once-gracious doors — now shabby with flaking paint — to shopkeepers and clerks and poor relations. My memory is of grass growing on avenues, and gardens gone wild, and faded drawing-rooms where cards or bagatelle were played. A Mrs Orpen came from such a house to hear the rugby internationals on our new Philips wireless, and stood when God Save the King was played, rigid as a ramrod, to my parents' bewildered amusement and the giggling of children. Keeping faith with the irretrievable past — no matter how comic a form it took — was often the hallmark of the dispossessed.

My memory, also, is of poverty in the back streets that was crueller and more claustrophobic than that which afflicted the Anglo-Irish. Children ran barefoot, men without work leaned on their half-doors, black-shawled women begged. From their hovels drifted the odour of their congested lives, blending with the ubiquitous turf smoke. They never ventured near the sea that was so close to them, but once a year, in August, the excursion trains brought the slums of Cork for a day out on the strand. A ragged mass of sharp-faced city urchins, the boys' heads cropped, the girls' infested, yelled among the breakwaters and forgot that they were hungry. When they had gone the promenade filled up again with those who strolled it, and then the sea came in and washed away the fleas. Was all of it another legacy of the past, as the grass growing on the avenue was, and a woman rising loyally for an anthem? No child of six or seven, which I was then, knows that such a question may be asked.

The nuns of the Loreto convent, where I was sent to school, may have asked it among themselves, but if they did they were not embittered by any conclusions reached. As one of the few Protestant children in that confident Catholic world I was treated fondly, and recall neither prejudice nor attempts at religious influence. We left the classroom during prayers and catechism, and during that time were the lay sisters' pets, plied with marzipan and other kitchen goodies. When my father was promoted, which meant moving to the West Cork town of Skibbereen and to a Protestant school, education was less pleasant.

The war years — the Emergency we called them — held time back. Out came the abandoned dog-cart, the pony and trap, the horse and cart. Long journeys were mulled over before engaged upon, and usually it was easier to stay where you were. The closed-in feeling of this isolated life was intensified by the authority of an increasingly priest-ridden society. The Censorship Board, directly influenced by the Church, examined for traces of sexual or religious laxity every book that entered the country, its attention often alerted by zealous Customs officials. Not then a source of much wickedness, films were nonetheless crudely chopped about. All this — with shoddy home-produced goods and desperate government schemes to lighten the economic bleakness — appeared to be the new Ireland. 'Where were you in 1916?' was a question endlessly hurled across the floor of the Dail, the preoccupation with the past now shifting its ground from history to remembered time.

I attended a variety of provincial schools and often, while leaving one town and settling down in another, went to no school at all for quite long periods. The cinema — or picture-house, as it was more popularly called — provided an influence that cut deeper, and has lasted longer, than schoolroom information about trade winds and the rhomboid. *Men with Wings, The Bride Walks Out, Meet Me in St Louis* combined with Trigger, Andy Hardy, and falling in love with Barbara Stanwyck, to cheer those wartime winters, while Lord Haw-Haw stirred things up on the radio. My sister's schoolgirl paperbacks stifled the tedium of doing nothing, and when that small library was exhausted there were detective stories set among the nightclubs of Mayfair or in sleeping Gloucestershire villages. The only available books about Ireland were *Jimín*, in Irish, at school, and *Knocknagow* by Charles Kickham, which I abandoned after the first paragraph.

My future, I believed, lay in some form of commerce, serving in a grocer's shop or a draper's, or as a bank clerk. I imagined myself, even with some excitement, weighing out half-pounds of rashers or measuring material by the yard; in a quiet moment settling down to yet another orange-covered Crime Club mystery; going to the pictures every time there was a change of programme.

★

Instead, when more time had passed and many mistakes been made, I became a writer of fiction and began — as all fiction-writers do — to refashion the real world, to pick over bits and pieces of experience and use anything that was useful. These essays are a small part of what has been left behind after all that.

EXCURSIONS IN THE
REAL WORLD

In County Cork

My EARLIEST MEMORIES are of County Cork: of sunshine and weeds in a garden at Mitchelstown, Civic Guards in the barracks next door, a tarred gate; of dark limestone steps in Youghal, and a backyard tap in Skibbereen. These three small towns, to the north, east and west of Cork City, have only slight, perfunctory claims to fame. A rare breed of spider is attracted to Mitchelstown's caves; its martyrs, of 1887, are not forgotten; more recently, processed cheese put it on the map. Youghal is where Sir Walter Ralegh lived, in Myrtle Lodge by the gates of St Mary's Protestant church. The *Skibbereen Eagle* warned a Russian Czar that it was watching his every move.

To the stranger they might be three towns anywhere in Ireland: big Catholic church, old Protestant graves, a cinema struggling on, haphazardly parked cars, turf smoke in the back streets, pubs and the Angelus, dancing on a Friday. But the county to which they belong has its own insistent idiosyncrasy, as marked in its changing landscape as in its singsong intonation. It is the county of the Blackwater and the Lee, spacious and unhurried, the most varied in Ireland. The lush farming land of neighbouring Limerick and Tipperary influences its northern boundaries. The Waterford coastline does not obediently change character when Waterford has finished with it. West Cork has been filched from Kerry.

Going back sets nostalgia right; time-worn impressions are corrected. Going back is a lesson in proportion, an exercise in give-and-take, more revelation than *déjà vu*. Sixty years on, Mitchelstown has a beaten look that memory has failed to register, its shops economically squat, its skyline humble beneath the mountains that make it seem as if someone has sat on it. The woman in the chemist's remembers my mother. The town's doing well, the proprietor of a drapery and footwear business says, but even so the jobs in the bacon factory and the creameries aren't enough to go round. All the time the population's increasing.

The same is true in nearby Mallow and Fermoy, but these are places with a past more evident to the eye than the martyrdom of tenant-farmers in 1887. The orderly garrison town that Fermoy once was marks it as firmly as the late-twentieth century does with the out-of-business Coffee Dock, the supermarkets and the filling stations. Mallow's Georgian elegance is still discernible beneath its crumbling stucco. All around for miles are the tree-studded meadows of the great estates where the Rakes of Mallow rampaged and hunted and shouted their heads off. Edmund Spenser looked out from Kilcolman Castle and, line by line, advanced his *Faerie Queene*. Had my family remained in Mitchelstown I would have been one of the small boys who were employed every summer to field the tennis-balls when they bounced out of court at nearby Bowen's Court.

The Rakes of Mallow belong in gardens now. A local poet writes, not of the vine-prop Elm, the Poplar never dry; but of the last train at Fermoy station, 1967. A bungalow replaces Bowen's Court. Yet the truth that Ireland is nowhere successful in shaking off its several pasts is as evident in this northern part of County Cork as it is in the west or down in the south-east, where the Blackwater slips into the sea.

The dark limestone steps I remember in Youghal belong to a narrow house, cocked up high, blank windows staring out to sea, valerian wild in every crevice where it can find a foothold. The house has a derelict look; it's a rooming establishment of some kind now, with rubbish piled in its flowerbeds and its small grass patch, an old mattress and two wet cardboard boxes, the springs of a pram. I remember scratching the sharp lid of a polish tin over the surface of the steps, making a sound that caused me to wince.

The characteristic quality of East Cork is in the flat ordinariness that stretches inland from Ballycotton Bay, in the village of Cloyne and the town of Midleton, in the estuary landscape of Youghal. It is an unassuming quality, a lack of drama, and this is in the people also — the Ronans, the Allens, the Kierans, the Cotters, the Ormonds. Yew thrives in the local soil, in fact gave Youghal its name. The Vikings took to the undemanding terrain.

Youghal itself is a town that hardly anyone dislikes. Once mildly fashionable as a watering-place, it attracted Pierrots and Punch and

Judy shows, and on its vast smooth sands old seaside artists painted garish pictures with coloured powders: peacocks and castles and women in hats, sometimes an annunciation. Beach pyjamas, often garish also, were on parade from June to August. A man called Tommy Atkins saved the life of a summer visitor, a woman who afterwards lay plump and unconscious on the sand in a blue bathing dress and a white rubber cap. Sometimes, in winter, the fishing boats did not come back.

The wooden breakwaters have rotted and are rotting still. The ferry that cost a penny doesn't operate any more. The railway station is a ruin, the promenade boarding-houses aren't there now because they're not what people want these days: the Pacific and the Atlantic, Sans Souci,

3

Clay Castle House. But the stubby little lighthouse is as it always was, whitely gleaming on the rocks.

There was a neat old woman who drove round in a wickerwork trap: Miss Goff of the ivy-covered cottage on the Lismore road. Old Zeb Miller, a canon of the Church of Ireland, gave children Glacier Mints long before children were ever told not to take sweets from a stranger. 'Feathery Ike, Feather Ike,' those same children chanted, 'give us a ride on your buttery bike!' The identity of Feathery Ike is lost, and no one in Youghal remembers Miss Goff or old Zeb Miller. But in the Moby Dick bar there is some recollection of the family born without fingers. The story is still told: how a boarding-house keeper of this town, a vigilant Orange mason, hacked at the praying hands of Virgins when he found himself in Belgian churches during the First World War, how later his children were born fingerless.

Youghal, smartly elegant in my memory, is tatty on a wet afternoon. A carful of German tourists crawls along the seafront, the misty beach is empty. Once, people pointed here and remarked: my eavesdroppings told of an afternoon love affair conducted on that brief promenade, he a married doctor, she a lady in disgrace. I see them now as I made them in my fascination: she is thin, and dressed in red, laughing, with pale long hair; he is Ronald Colman with a greyer moustache. He strides along the promenade with a walking-stick and a small black dog, she waits for him on a seat. They smile at one another; defiantly he touches her hand. Their conversation is beautiful; they are breathtaking in their sinning. They are the world's most exciting people.

In St Mary's church on this damp afternoon a film crew are setting up their gear. In the vestry there are photographs of previous rectors, among them Canon Darling, good at tennis in 1934, who accidentally ignited a box of matches when meaning only to light a cigarette, whose cat sipped whiskey from his glass and staggered drunkenly about. The camera crew wear bright anoraks, but speak in low voices, as is fitting in these surroundings. A coffin rests on a trolley in front of the altar steps, a candle in a massive candlestick at each corner. The varnish of the coffin gleams, high-lighting the yellow wood. Such hefty candles, in this Protestant church, do not look right.

It is the most impressive parish church in Ireland. It used to be said that there were holes specially carved in the masonry, through which lepers could watch and take part in the services, but they do not seem to exist now and presumably never did. But the claim sounds good, and in more easygoing times no one bothered to look.

'An uphill struggle,' the clergyman complains, referring to the problems of old buildings and keeping everything up. He's dressed to take a service, and I wonder who has died. In fact, no one has: the yellow coffin's empty. 'Some kind of documentary,' the obliging cleric explains, his tone of voice suggesting there has been a fee. 'I wonder if I should tell them those candles shouldn't be there?'

A Wall of Death used to come to Youghal, and a man who pitched knives at his wife. He covered her in brown paper and made her stand against an old door, erected among the sand dunes. Girls screamed and cried out don't look. Afterwards the man's wife came round with a cap for coppers. There were only a few cuts on her and they'd all healed long ago. The annual Amusements came, and still do: bumper cars and roundabouts and games of chance, swing-boats and the Big Dipper. The Wall of Death was the best, the roar of the motorcycle to attract the crowds, the rickety circular wall, the woman standing on the pillion, a red scarf streaming from her smile.

The film makers are in the cinema now. The Regal it's called, it used to be something else; Horgan's, known for its fleas, was just across the street. The men who run the Regal — the projectionist and Tom, son of the proprietor of the distant past — speak of a renaissance. They have figures at their fingertips, what the latest *Indiana Jones* grossed at the box offices of America, how *Back to the Future 2* is doing. 'You knew the old hall?' Tom asks, and I affirm that, recalling this Regal's predecessor, the one that burnt down, as cinemas so often did. Jack Hulbert and Cicely Courtneidge were seen in *Round the Washtub* there, and a film with Jimmy O'Dea in which someone was shot by telephone. The chat goes on until the film crew call for silence. The lights dim, softening away the grubby seats and cigarette-burnt carpet. Ireland in wartime appears on the screen.

Youghal is bigger than once it was, its attractions different: seafood and discos, a decent cup of coffee. The quays are cleaner, the fishermen fewer, the Devonshire Arms has had another lick of paint. Behind the town, in a henhouse on the old back road, a man shot himself. This man's life was hell, it was whispered, and the henhouse developed an eeriness that the chatter of birds accentuated. The King of England died, that old bearded face in the *Daily Sketch*, the funeral service on the wireless. Another man died, a man who used to come quite often to our house, who had the habit of very finely chopping up his salad. And the woman we bought herrings from died. But all this death seemed quite in order at the time, except for the violence in the henhouse.

Youghal itself died in a way, for yellow furniture vans — Nat Ross of Cork — carted our possessions off, westward through Cork itself and through the town people called Clonakilty-God-Help-Us, through untidy Bandon, to Skibbereen, the back of beyond. The landscape becomes more ragged on that journey. Gorse grows well. Speckled rock-surfaces break out in the patchwork of fields. Once, the country-women of West Cork wore strangely hooded black cloaks as they walked these roads and lanes or sat in their donkey-butts. They greeted you from the shadowy depths, their easy laughter dispelling the suggestion of the sinister that this dress evoked. To this day, on a Sunday, their menfolk pitch heavy metal bowls along the same roads, laying wagers and marking with a sod torn from a ditch the length achieved by each. When a car appears they wave it on; the tourists are a hazard now.

A grey figure still marks the heart of Skibbereen, a statue of the Maid of Erin. It's in the way, but has been decreed by referendum to remain. Around it the shops are modest for the most part, the banks big, the bars frequent: a good business town, my father used to say. Memory focusses here, the dredged-up images are clearer. Horses and carts in the narrow streets, with milk churns for the creamery. On fair-days farmers with sticks standing by their animals, their shirts clean for the occasion, without collar or tie. A smell of whiskey, and sawdust and stout and dung. Pots of geraniums among chops and ribs in the small windows of butchers' shops. A sun-burnt poster, advertising the arrival of Duffy's Circus a year ago.

It was a mile and a half, the journey to school through the town, past Driscoll's sweetshop and Murphy's Medical Hall, and Power's drapery, where you could buy oilcloth as well as dresses. You made the journey home again at three. By three on fair-days the buying and selling was over, the publicans' takings safely banked, the dung sliding towards the gutters. If you had money you spent it on liquorice pipes or stuff for making lemonade, which was delicious if you ate it just as it was. The daughters of Power's drapery sometimes had money. But they were always well ahead, on bicycles because they were well-to-do. On fair-days their mother drove them in her Hillman because of the dung.

In the grocers' shops the big-jawed West Cork women buy flour and sausages and tins of plums, and trade their baskets of turkey eggs. E. O'Donovan, undertaker, still sells ice-cream and chocolate. The brass plate of Redmond O'Regan, solicitor, once awkwardly high, is now below eye-level, and Shannon's bakery has a café, where commercial travellers hurry through their cups of tea or coffee. Mr Dwyer, who bred smooth-haired fox-terriers, used to serve in Shannon's, expertly tying up pounds of sugar and tea in grey paper-bags. We bought a dog from him once, an animal called Dano who became infatuated with our cat.

The door beside the Methodist church, once green, is purple. The church, small and red-brick, stands behind high iron railings and gates, with gravel in front of it. Beyond the door that used to be green is the dank passage that leads to Miss Willoughby's schoolroom, where first I learnt that the world is not an easy-going place. Miss Willoughby was stern and young, in love with the cashier from the Provincial Bank. Like the church beside her schoolroom, she was Methodist and there burnt in her breast an evangelical spirit which stated that we, her pupils, except for her chosen few, must somehow be made less wicked than we were. Her chosen few were angels of a kind, their handwriting blessed, their compositions a gift from God. I was not among them.

On the gravel in front of the red-brick church I vividly recall Miss Willoughby. Terribly, she appears. Severe and beautiful, she pedals against the wind on her huge black bicycle. 'Someone laughed during prayers,' her stern voice accuses, and you feel at once that it was you, although you know it wasn't. *V. poor* she writes in your headline book when you've done your best to reproduce, four times, perfectly, *Pride goeth before destruction.*

As I stand on the gravel, her evangelical eyes seem again to dart over me without pleasure. Once I took the valves out of the tyres of her bicycle. Once I looked in her answer book. 'Typical,' her spectre says. 'Typical, to come prying.' I am late, I am stupid. I cannot write twenty sentences on A Day in the Life of an Old Shoe, I cannot do simple arithmetic or geography, I am always fighting with Jasper Swanton. I move swiftly on the gravel, out on to the street and into the bar of the

Eldon Hotel: in spectral form or otherwise, Miss Willoughby will not be there.

'Place of the little boats' Skibbereen is. Its river is the Ilen; the sea's just down the road. Its people are Wolfes and Woods and Hosfords, Dukelows and Vickerys, O'Donovans, O'Mahonys, Cronins, Hogans. Beyond the town the coastline's all bits and pieces, broken-off islands, bays within bays, slivers of peninsula. Turf bogs and hills, rocky land, marshy land, useless land, here and there an acre of grass: the Wild West of Cork begins beyond Ballydehob. A railway used to run by the roadside, with a once-a-day cow-catcher to the village of Schull.

Along the jagged coast is Mizen Head and Dunmanus Bay, Durrus, Bantry, Whiddy Island, tropical Glengarriff. Inland, to the right, St Finbarr built a church on an islet at Gougane Barra, the source of the River Lee, which meanders its way on to Cork City. Here the disparate elements of the county merge. The natives speak swiftly in the city, but visiting country people keep their end up and are, in turn, never under-estimated.

Going to Cork, the journey to the city, was once the nicest thing of all. Fifty-two miles in the old Renault, thirty miles an hour because my mother wouldn't permit speed. On St Stephen's Day to the pantomime in the Opera House, and on some other occasion to *White Horse Inn*, which my father had heard was good. In Cork my appendix was removed because Cork's surgical skill was second to none. In Cork my tongue was cut to rid me of my incoherent manner of speaking. To Cork, every day of my childhood, I planned to run away.

Twice a year perhaps, on Saturday afternoons, there was going to Cork to the pictures. Clark Gable and Myrna Loy in *Too Hot to Handle*. *Mr Deeds Goes to Town*. No experience in my whole childhood, and no memory, has remained as deeply etched as these escapes to the paradise that was Cork. Nothing was more lovely or more wondrous than Cork itself, with its magnificent array of cinemas: the Pavilion, the Savoy, the Palace, the Ritz, the Lee, and Hadji Bey's Turkish Delight factory. Tea in Thompson's or the Savoy, the waitresses with silver-plated tea-pots and buttered bread and cakes, and other people eating fried eggs with rashers and chipped potatoes at half-past four in the afternoon. The sheer sophistication of Thompson's or the Savoy could never be adequately conveyed to a friend in Skibbereen who had not had the good fortune to experience it. The Gentlemen's lavatory in the Victoria Hotel had to be seen to be believed, the Munster Arcade left you gasping. For ever and for ever you could sit in the middle stalls of the Pavilion watching Claudette Colbert, or Spencer Tracy as a priest, and the earthquake in San Francisco. And for ever afterwards you could sit while a green-clad waitress carried the silver-plated tea-pot to you, with cakes and buttered bread. All around you was the clatter of life and of the city, and men of the world conversing, and girls' laughter tinkling. Happiness was everywhere.

(1971)

The Strand

YOU CAN WALK along the strand all the way from Ardmore to the derelict one-storey Georgian house on the cliff. You pass Ballyquin on the way, a little cove that has a car park now. The sand is smooth and damp, here and there marbled with grey, or dusty dry, depending on whether you choose to walk by the sea or closer to the cliffs. There are shrimps and anemones in the rock pools, and green slithery seaweed as you pass the rocky places by. The cliffs are clay, easy game for the encroaching winter waves. Washed timber and plastic bottles are the flotsam of the shingle.

A woman pushes a bicycle, the buckets that hang from its handlebars heavy with seafood from the rocks. A horse and cart carries gravel or seaweed back to Ballyquin. In the nineteen thirties this strand was always empty, except on the rare days when the dark figure of a priest was seen, suddenly there out of nowhere, clambering down the cliff-face. Clothes were weighed down with a stone and then he ran naked to the sea.

Inland a little way, not always visible from the strand, is Ballyquin House, four-square and architecturally simple, cream-washed when the O'Reillys lived there. Mrs O'Reilly, a widow, attired always in black, was a woman whose unobtrusive presence called for, but did not demand, respect. All the old decencies were in the woman that Mrs O'Reilly was: you hardly had to look at her to know she would rather not live at all than live dubiously, in some mean-spirited way. Her two children, Biddy and Henry, were in their early twenties. Her brother, a silent man who kept his hat on, worked the farm. An old uncle — known as Blood-an'-Ouns because he so often used the expression — got drunk in Ardmore every Corpus Christi, but otherwise did not touch a drop.

Henry O'Reilly was known locally as the laziest man in Ireland, but in my childhood opinion he was also the nicest. Red-haired and already becoming bulky, he took me with him on the cart to the creamery and on the way back we would stop at a crossroads half-and-half — a shop that was a grocery as well as a public house. He had a bottle of stout himself, and bought me a lemonade and biscuits. He would settle his elbows on the counter, exchanging whatever news there was with the woman who served us. 'Give the boy another mineral,' he'd say, and he'd order another packet of biscuits for me, or a Cadbury's bar. Eventually the horse would take us slowly on, lingering through the sunshine, Henry O'Reilly having a nap, the reins in my charge. Most of the day it took, to go to the creamery and back.

Henry O'Reilly made me an aeroplane, nailing together a few scraps of wood, which he then painted white. He showed me how to snare a rabbit and how to shoot one. When I was eight or so I weeded a field of mangolds with him, a task that didn't require much energy because we stopped whenever a new story began, and Henry O'Reilly went in for stories: about his ancestors, and '98, and the Troubles, the Black and Tans, the time Michael Collins passed near by. At twelve o'clock we returned to the farmhouse and sat down in the kitchen to a meal of potatoes, which were tumbled out on to a newspaper in the centre of the table.

The O'Reillys' land stretched right to the cliff edge, but the O'Reillys rarely ventured on to the strand, as country people who live by the sea so often don't. There were cows to milk, and feed to be boiled for the hens, and crops to be harvested, the churns of milk delivered. The front door of the house was never opened, the rooms on either side of it and the bedrooms above only entered when dusting took place. Gladstone hung in severe majesty over a mantelpiece, eyed by the Virgin above the door. Hall and stairway were embellished with further reminders, faith kept, thanks given.

There is a glen where the strand ends, separating the land that was once the O'Reillys' from woods that have become dense. And there, much closer to the cliff edge than the O'Reillys', is the derelict house. The woods stretch for miles behind it and somewhere in the middle of them lived a man with rheumy eyes called Paddy Lyndon. In a tumbled-down outbuilding there was an old motor-car with brass headlamps — one of the first, Paddy Lyndon averred, that had taken to the roads in Ireland. 'Are you sober, Paddy?' Henry O'Reilly would always greet Paddy Lyndon when they met, an enquiry that received no response.

Glencairn House the derelict place was called when first I knew it fifty years ago. It was owned then by an Englishman who'd left Ireland during the Troubles and only rarely returned — a Mr Fuge who'd built a dream house, not knowing that dreams are not to be trusted. 'As good a man as ever stood on two feet,' Paddy Lyndon said. 'A man that never owed a debt.' Through the cracks of the efficiently boarded windows nothing could be distinguished in the darkness that kept the rooms' secrets. A briar rose trailed through a patch of garden, gone as wild as the surrounding gorse. I liked the mystery of this good Englishman who'd left his property in Paddy Lyndon's charge, who only stayed for twenty minutes when he came back. 'There's stories about Fuge I could tell you,' Henry O'Reilly said, but he never did because he never got round to making them up.

But it is the sea, not houses or people, that dominates the strand. To the sea, and the sand and rocks that receive it, belong the images you carry with you when you pass on to the woody slopes of the glen, and the barley fields. The waves call the tune of the place, in a murmur or a passionate crescendo. There's salt on the inland air, and seagulls strut the furrows.

Jellyfish float in when they're in a mood for it. Once in a while there's a trawler on the horizon. The sea on the turn's the best, the sand left perfect or waiting to be doused. It's easier to skim pebbles over the water when it's unruffled — as it was the time I nearly drowned, causing panic one hot afternoon.

Two generations on, the shells are as they've always been; so are the paw-prints of a dog. The dog has a branch of brown seaweed trailing from its jaws, and takes no notice when he's called. People nod as they pass, or say hullo. Children build castles and watch them being washed away, old men paddle. A primus stove splutters. It's out of the question that a naked priest will run into the sea.

Still no one lives in the derelict house. The boards that once so curtly covered the windows, a kind of packing case around the house, have fallen away. You can see the rooms now, but if ever there was furniture all of it has gone. The wall beside the avenue has collapsed.

The O'Reillys' farmhouse is different too. Years ago Biddy made her way to Chicago, Henry married into Ardmore. Mrs O'Reilly and her

brother, the old man too, are long since dead. The house is no longer in the family, the land is differently farmed.

There is no nostalgia here, only remembered facts — and the point that passing time has made: the strand is still the strand, taking change and another set of *mores* in its stride, as people and houses cannot. While you walk its length, there is something comforting in that.

(1992)

Kitty

'WHY HAVE YOU shut the door, Kitty?'
    'Because of the boys, ma'am.'
'What have they been doing, Kitty?'
'Setting the house on fire, ma'am.'

Kitty wasn't young any more, or seemed not to be, and she'd never been pretty. She had eyes that were always blinking and teeth my brother called 'stormy' — a mouthful of enormous white crags, constantly bared in laughter or anger. When I was eight and my brother six we particularly enjoyed lighting fires and would indulge this inclination on the kitchen floor when Kitty was left in charge of us. While she was changing into her afternoon black we would carefully arrange newspaper and kindling before putting a match to them, and she'd return to the kitchen to find it full of smoke and flames. Later she'd stand terrified in the hall while we paraded through the house with lengths of flaring bog-wood held triumphantly above our heads, as often as not dressed up in some of her clothes. When we couldn't afford Woodbines in Mrs O'Brien's shop just down the road we rolled up damp paper and smoked it instead. Kitty's only weapon was to shut the kitchen door. The kitchen door was never shut as a rule.

Severe punishment followed, but we never learned a lesson from it. The day my father drove the fifty-two miles to Cork to have his teeth out he made us promise we'd be good, hinting at a reward. My mother, who could never resist Cork, went with him, and when they returned he came into our bedroom and asked us if we'd behaved well. We replied that we had. He produced two gold-coloured metal pencil-sharpeners, but before he could give them to us Kitty appeared in the doorway.

'Indeed they haven't, sir,' she contradicted shrilly. 'They've never been worse, sir. They called names over the wall at Mr Hayes, sir. They took raisins and syrup, sir.'

'Oh, now,' my father began.

'They brought tinkers into the kitchen, sir. They had them sitting down in the drawing-room.'

The pencil-sharpeners were withdrawn and were never given to us. My father looked at us without saying anything.

Kitty was the nearest we ever came to having an old retainer. For the time she was with us she was part of the family, yet her life — as the life of any general maid tended to be at that time — was solitary. She was permitted liberties: when she bought new clothes, which wasn't often, she ordered a selection to be sent to the house from three or four drapers' shops. Vast piles of coats, skirts or hats would accumulate on the dining-room table and Kitty would try on garment after garment while my mother — gratefully killing an empty morning or afternoon — helped her to choose.

But in spite of all that the two were not companions in any close sense, for no matter what confidences were shared there remained the gulf that inevitably separates mistress and servant. Kitty was there to work — in the kitchen and the bedrooms, the dining-room, the drawing-room, in the hall and on the stairs and landings. In return for modest wages, it is hardly an exaggeration to say that she gave the greater part of her being.

The lone general maid was a familiar fixture in any household that could afford one. She was to be found above stairs in public houses and grocers' shops, in the terraced dwellings of clerks and small-time bookmakers. 'Have they a maid?' was a question often asked, the answer supplying instant social status. Maids' uniforms were illustrated in drapers' catalogues, blue or pink for the mornings, black or brown later on. 'Is she clean?' was a query made of previous employers, and: 'Is she honest?' Smarter households had more than one, called parlour maids, and a cook, and a weekly woman for the floors and washing. All that made a difference, not just where status was concerned, but to the maids themselves. There was companionship in the kitchen, meals taken together, the foibles of the family whispered over. 'Is it a fast day for you, Kitty?' my mother would enquire and if it was, Kitty would fry herself an egg, her isolation again compounded. She went to Mass, we to church. Yet she never hung a holy picture in her bedroom: that would have been presumptuous.

Her existence was lightened by bits of gossip. Awestruck, she would repeat the latest about Jack Doyle and Movita when they'd visited Bantry or Dunmanway. Doyle was a once-renowned boxer, now a general entertainer on small-town stages; Movita was declared to be a 'film star', and certainly dressed like one. They were mild hell-raisers, one story being that finding a hotel full when they wished to spend a night in it, Doyle drove a honeymoon couple from their bed and pursued them in their nightclothes through the streets.

Recalled with equal pleasure was the night the French hypnotist reduced a hardware merchant's assistant to a state of unconsciousness and couldn't bring him back. 'The poor fellow went home thinking he was a chicken,' Kitty never tired of repeating, tears of delight streaming on her roughened cheeks. In the end a medical hypnotist from Dublin had to rescue the youth from the tower of the Protestant church, where his confusion had led him. But even though he later managed to shake off the delusion that he was a chicken he was never, according to Kitty, the same again.

A wrestler called O'Mahoney, whom she confessed she'd never seen in the flesh, was her hero, but for the most part her interests and her preferences went unmentioned. She instigated little in her life: experience was what happened to her. Our dog Dano once followed Kitty to Mass, barking at her in the church when she tried to ignore him. She afterwards retailed the episode in detail, stuttering through her laughter, her huge teeth stormier than ever. 'The commotion there was, ma'am! Father Tracy with the Host, and Dano rampaging, and the men at the back whistling to get him out!'

She courted such embarrassment. At Duffy's Circus one of the clowns sat in her lap while everyone applauded. A man who came to paint the hall tried to kiss her, putting his arms around her under a ladder. A drunk sang a song for her when she was buying chops in Bridge Street. Her reaction in these awkward moments was always the same: red as a sunset, she would laugh wildly.

She had a friend, another maid in the town. On Sunday afternoons they would cycle out on the Cork road for a couple of miles and then cycle back again. They went together to Women's

Confraternity, once a year to Piper's Travelling Entertainments, occasionally to the pictures. No man ever took Kitty out: she didn't have the looks for dancehalls, or for courting in hedges; the housepainter who tried something on was a married man in his fifties, father of nine.

Had she not become our maid she would have remained at home, in a cottage near Ballycotton, an extra mouth to feed. Meagre though it was, the money she earned was something, and at least when she closed the door of her attic room she was private while she slept. A chipped, white-painted washstand, with a narrow cupboard and dressing-table to match, a single discarded hearthrug on the boards of the floor, constituted that bedroom world, where rosary beads were told and Hail Marys repeated, and all Kitty's washing of herself took place. She was woken at half-past six by the rattle of the alarm clock that summoned her to the first of her tasks — the lighting of the range. The kitchen became hers only in the evenings, when the day's work was done, after earthenware hot-water jars had been placed in every bed, and the fire in the range had been damped down after the day's last meal. One of the armless wooden chairs was drawn out from the table and Kitty darned or read *Ireland's Own*, or just sat there with Dano and the cat.

Eventually she gave notice and returned to her family in Ballycotton. My mother said the obstreperousness of my brother and myself had unhinged her. There followed a long procession of unsatisfactory maids. One of them didn't return after a night's dancing at a roadside platform, another wouldn't get up in the mornings, others couldn't be trained. 'Well, I'd better go out and look for a maid,' my mother used to say when she found herself without one, and would set off at random into the countryside to see what the cottages had to offer.

Years later, Kitty was written to in Ballycotton and informed that my brother and myself had at last acquired sense. We were older and would soon be going away to boarding-school. So Kitty made the long journey to where we now lived, and my brother and I met her at the railway station. I wheeled her bicycle through the streets, my brother balanced her brown cardboard suitcase on the carrier. It seemed like a lovely town, Kitty said, blinking excitedly as she looked about her. We said it was a great place.

'Oh, that's a lovely room!' she exclaimed a little later, surveying her bedroom from the door. The same white washstand was there, a little more chipped than it had been, the same narrow cupboard and dressing-table, the same discarded hearthrug. From the window there was a view of a turf-merchant's yard.

(1992)

Field of Battle

MY FATHER WAS a big, healthy-looking man with a brown bald head and brown tobacco fingers. He liked to tell stories rather than jokes — stories about people or events that amused him. He smoked Sweet Aftons, drank anything he was offered, and had a flair for picking winners, always turning first to the sports pages of the *Irish Times* and the *Cork Examiner*. As he advanced in his career as a bank official he became skilled at guessing which farmers to lend money to. He was popular with the townspeople he lived among, popular with country people because he understood them.

My mother was tiny, capricious and beautiful, firm of purpose, fiery and aloof, with a sharp tongue, and an eccentric sense of humour that often took you by surprise. She had a faint Northern Irish accent, and used to say she supported the North when in the South and the South (the Free State as it was then called) when in the North. She was a great reader: Philip Gibbs, Francis Brett Young, A.J. Cronin, Robert Hichens. In the succession of small towns where we lived she borrowed their books, in brown-paper jackets from the nuns at the convent, or from a branch of the Argosy circulating library, usually to be found at the back of a sweetshop. She had a weakness for Fred Astaire and Ginger Rogers.

My father hardly read at all and although he willingly accompanied my mother to *Top Hat* and *The Story of Vernon and Irene Castle*, his preference was for gangster adventures featuring Edward G. Robinson or James Cagney. They agreed about the Thin Man series, but to their three children it often seemed that they agreed about little else. Accord was short-lived, increasingly so as the years went by.

What children of a marriage rarely witness is the nature of the love that brought the whole thing — themselves included — into being in the first place. The marriage of parents is almost always mysterious:

19

the sensual elements scarcely bear thinking about, the romantic past can only be guessed at, and all such curiosity invariably comes too late.

What inadequately fills the vacuum now is a sun-browned photograph of a young man in plus-fours with hair brushed straight back. He stands by a motorcycle and there's a misty image of the girl in the sidecar, her face mostly turned away. She disliked being photographed — an odd distaste in a beautiful woman. He didn't mind: in other snapshots he is at the wheel of an open-hooded Morris Cowley; striding across the square in Mountbellew; lighting a cigarette. They are together, newly engaged, two in a family group: his white-bearded father and upright handsome mother, his brothers and sisters and unidentified friends, all sitting on the grass at Millbrook, the County Roscommon farm which due to some misfortune was soon to slip out of the family's grasp. Honeymooning, they are together again, strolling on the promenade at Bray.

They met in Dundalk, he a bank clerk in the Bank of Ireland, she the first 'lady clerk' ever to be employed by the Ulster Bank. Their backgrounds were not dissimilar: she, too, came of farming stock, from the apple country of Armagh, a small farm near the village of Loughgall. There wasn't much money on either side, none at all to spare for this marriage, for any kind of dowry or for a few sticks of furniture: love and optimism were all it had.

Both were charming in different ways, and all their lives remained so. But their charming of one another, their pride in one another, their pleasing of one another: in later years it was hard to believe any of that had ever been there. What had lasted was a kind of rivalry that once, perhaps, was playful. Otherwise no effort was made, there was no give and take. Speculation charts a marital progression: from being lovers to becoming enemies in love, and then that rivalry turning sour.

The cold facts, all that is known, tell nothing: what happened, or did not happen, is private territory, a disappointment guarded in life and death. They made no bones about their shattered relationship, yet in all the quarrels that exploded, in all the accusations and recriminations, in all the brooding silences, there never was a clue to the truth that lay at the root of its failure.

In the places where they lived together, shackled within convention — in Dundalk, Mountbellew, Mitchelstown, Youghal, Skibbereen,

Tipperary, Enniscorthy, Portlaoise, Galway — indifference drifted into irritation, into hatred in the end. Yet now and again, as though in mockery, there were faint echoes of what had once so briefly been, hints at least of a companionship, if never of the passion that had burnt away. Once in a while, not often, there was a visit to a race-meeting together, a variation of the Saturday-afternoon journey to one of the cinemas in Cork. Parties were attended in one another's company, and parties given. One summer the family spent four or five weeks in a remote bay along the Waterford coast, he making the daily journey back to the bank in Youghal when his own holiday came to an end. Tents, including a marquee, were hired, and erected in a field on a cliff. Chests of drawers and dressing-tables, beds, chairs, oil stove and wireless set, were conveyed in a borrowed lorry to the cliff-top site. Camping wasn't common in those days, and had a pioneering feel to it. Milk had to be fetched from a distant farmhouse, and baskets of potatoes and peas, and water from a spring. There was a sense of enjoyment about the adventure, which stretched a skin over whatever wounds there were, and while that summer lasted there was a fragile harmony.

In the evenings the big paraffin lamps were lit in the marquee and a record played on the wind-up gramophone: *Red Sails in the Sunset*, *The Isle of Capri*. He set snares for rabbits and never caught any; she laughed at him and he didn't take offence, getting his own back by trying to take a photograph of her. But even so they never addressed one another with endearments, or by their Christian names. And suddenly, out of nowhere, something would go wrong and silence would cut the chatter short. Halcyon days could not be counted on. Nothing could.

The divide widened: the last good family memories are of that cliff-top habitation and the sea below. In the bleakness that possessed the marriage all the love was given to its children, who would happily have settled for less. Only they were optimistic now, hoping without encouragement that miraculously everything would change, that when a silence of months came to an end the communication that replaced it would not be short-lived. But it always was.

The autumn following that last summer dragged by, then winter and spring. Morosely, he worked the hand-pump in the yard, twice a day conveying water to the tanks in the loft. On Sunday mornings he carried tea to her in bed, but no word was exchanged. Gregariously he went about his business, and frequented more bars than once he had. She took up leather-work.

Their spirit was not broken. Both laughed a lot, but differently, and not in one another's company. Both were clever, but in different ways. Both were perceptive, but did not share the nature of their perception. Perhaps she was too complicated for a simple man, he too undemanding for a demanding woman. Yet all this might have been overcome, and often is in marriage. What could not be was that she had borne three children and was left with no further purpose. He was making his way; for her, as he did so, there was the claustrophobia of small-town existence. Her frustration was that she was the victim of circumstance, his that he could do nothing about it.

In September 1939, soon after the war broke out, there was the move from Skibbereen to Tipperary, and life became even more confined. The cinemas of Cork, where she had eased her mind, were no longer within reach. Gone, too, were its clothes shops, which she loved, and late-night suppers while the voices of Nelson Eddy and Jeanette MacDonald still echoed. Without petrol, there was no escape, without love no release.

He strolled down the street to Dobbin's Hotel and to the club next door where he played cards. When he returned in the middle of the night the sound of quarrelling would begin in their children's dreams and then become real. He joined the Local Defence Force and would disappear into the Galtee mountains on manoeuvres. Another excuse for drinking, she said.

Christmas was a time when the fragments of the family uneasily came together. He still sent to Switzer's in Dublin for scents and cosmetics he had seen advertised in their catalogue, and these would be waiting for her at breakfast on Christmas morning. She still bought him things herself, scarves and ties mainly, sometimes a pullover. Gratitude for these gifts would be conveyed in a roundabout way, through admiration of the articles received. But as the years went on all that broke down: Christmas became a bad time because of the nature of the occasion, because of the extra drink or two in Dobbin's and because, for her, the Argosy Library wasn't up to much, restricted in what it could offer because of the war, not enough to see her through those empty festive days. There was a dearth of social life. Tipperary's one small cinema burnt down.

She took to creating drama out of unpromising splinters of everyday life. One of these was a love-affair between a clergyman and a lady doctor, both of them middle-aged and married to other people. They had met when the former was summoned to administer the last rites at a deathbed, the latter having already done what she could. Waiting in the house for the inevitable death, the erring couple fell in love, and the rest had to do with the rector's car being observed late at night in places where it should not be. The town now was Enniscorthy, and County Wexford tongues — Catholic as well as Protestant — joyfully wagged. The respectable caught with their dirty linen in disarray — medicine and the Church canoodling in the back of a Ford V-8 — was relished with a vengeance. The unfortunate cleric's churchwardens carted him around the parish, from house to house, urging his parishioners to give him a talking to. 'As good as the pictures,' my mother remarked. 'As good as Warwick Deeping.' But such real-life drama was rare, and as time went on and removal vans came again and again, this rootless life increasingly took a toll on its own account. For almost half a lifetime new friends hadn't had a chance to become old ones; there'd been endless adjustment to different houses and surroundings, yet another wearying beginning in place after place. Behind the lace curtains that had been altered to fit windows all over the south of Ireland life stumbled on, until it stumbled to a halt.

Abruptly they separated and did not ever meet again. They had stayed together for the sake of the children, and the children were now grown up. It might have been better had they not done so, but in retrospect there is something gallant about their efforts to hold together the family their one-time love had brought into existence. Their perseverance was full of a self-sacrifice that was not apparent while they were making it; and there was a courageous honesty in their refusal to hide from their children the plight their marriage had become. They did not cover up; there was no hypocrisy.

My mother died a crippled and unhappy woman, in 1965. On a freezing snowy day her body was conveyed from Dublin to County Armagh and buried beside her father's in the small Church of Ireland graveyard at Loughgall. All the way along the route, eighty or so miles, people crossed themselves as the hearse went by, and since Catholics had always respected the firm Protestant she'd been it seemed apt enough. Apt, too, that the husband she had married forty-four years ago wasn't there.

He died ten years later, of a heart attack while he was drying his hands. He was eighty-four and still attending race-meetings.

'It was all my fault,' she said in a vague moment towards the end of her life. He might have said the same, but I doubt that that was where the truth lay. They were victims of their innocence when chance threw them together and passion beguiled them, leaving them to live with a mistake and to watch their field of battle expanding with each day that passed. They gave their love to their children and were loved in return, fiercely, unwaveringly. But not for a moment could that heal the wounds they carried to their graves.

(1992)

Miss Quirke

LONG BEFORE I was sent away to boarding-school there was Miss Quirke. She was the ultimate successor of the nuns in Youghal, Miss Willoughby in Skibbereen, and the national school in Tipperary.

My mother declared the last named was educationally inadequate and she was probably right. While attending it I was entered for a nationwide Church of Ireland examination in religious knowledge, and assured beyond doubt that this would result in my acquiring a silver medal. With a boy called Hadnett, I sat for a whole morning in Canon Stringer's study in the rectory, plied with ginger beer by the elderly clergyman and his wife. My knowledge of the Bible was scant: I was unable to supply information about the engrafted word that saves souls or Shimri the son of Shemaiah, or what happened when Zipporah took a sharp stone. In the end Canon Stringer told me a thing or two and I wrote them down. Then he left us on our own and Hadnett, who had finished and was examining the contents of a drawer, told me another thing or two, which I wrote down also. Unfortunately Hadnett knew as little as I did and when the same misunderstandings were later noted as emanating from the same rectory we were both disqualified. My mother said the whole thing was a farce and a yardstick of the school's ineptitude when it came to assessing its pupils' potential. A failed Christian brother, at a loose end in the town, was engaged to come daily to an upstairs room of our house in Main Street and instruct my brother and myself. John Joe he was called, but he turned out not to be suitable, mainly because after a week or so he declared he couldn't manage on the wages. So John Joe left and Miss Quirke replaced him.

She had been found in a farmhouse at Oola, a few miles from Tipperary, where she'd been vaguely waiting for something to happen, as many a country girl was at that time. Fair-haired, pink-cheeked, she was probably little more than a schoolgirl, although she seemed old, and wise. Her soft, solemn smile and calm voice, her unhurried movements, her modesty, her confidence, all supported this impression.

Every morning she rode in on her BSA, a breath of fresh air from Oola. Often she came with brambles or sprigs of birch and oak snipped from the hedges. These were arranged on the table in front of my brother and myself and we were instructed to paint them in watercolours. Poster paint was produced; ink was mixed with glue and patterns made with combs cut from cardboard. We were told about the continental Sunday, and the Guillotine and the Champs-Élysées. We were shown pictures of *baguettes* and *ficelles*, so very different from our own dreary pan loaves and turn-overs. Joan of Arc and Niall of the Nine Hostages were rescued from the dust that had years ago settled on them. Mathematical subjects were less distasteful than they had been. Even geography had its moments, though admittedly not many.

Patiently, without anger, errors and aberrations were corrected, a Relief nib forever dipping into the bottle of Stephens' red ink Miss Quirke uncorked every morning when she sat down. Her composure was startling the more it was in evidence, her knowledge seemingly endless. She knew why rain came down in drops. She knew the names of clouds, and how to bind a book, and the exact town in America where the electric chair had been invented, and by whom, and whose life it had first claimed. She knew the names of the Chicago gangsters, and that the story of William Tell was a myth, and that it was all nonsense about St George and the dragon. She described the Famine ships that had taken the starving Irish across the Atlantic, how every day more bodies had been dropped over the side, how only the fortunate had survived. She read *Lorna Doone* aloud.

Before she arrived one morning my brother and I placed a Hornby train engine in the drawer of the table at which our lessons were conducted. We attached a string to one of its levers and trailed the string through a hole bored in the bottom of the drawer, through a cup-hook screwed into the floor beneath, along the skirting-board and beneath the door. At eleven o'clock, when tea and Everyday biscuits were brought to Miss Quirke, we were released from the upstairs room for ten minutes or so. On the landing the string was jerked, the lever released, and the clockwork engine began its drone in the drawer. Overcome by our wit, we jammed our fists into our mouths, imagining her flustered bewilderment once she had recovered from the shock. When we re-entered the room, still red-faced from sniggering, Miss Quirke was reading the *Irish Independent*, as she always was when we returned from our ten minutes. She was smiling over Gussie Goose and Curly Wee. 'Awfully good today,' she said, and read it out.

One Saturday afternoon she was in the back row of the balcony at the new Excel Cinema, with a man. This interested us greatly, and we kept turning round to see if they were cuddling, but it was impossible to make out anything in the dark. The man wore a suit and had a moustache, and was offering her a cigarette when the lights went up. We watched them mounting their bicycles and riding off. 'Was he your brother?' we planned to enquire, nonchalantly, on Monday morning, but we never did because she mentioned the encounter first, saying that the film we'd seen — Mickey Rooney as the young Thomas Edison — was historically inaccurate, and proceeded to adjust it for us.

Miss Quirke was an influence for no more than a few months, but the memory of her wisdom insistently lingers. When the news came that we were to move from Tipperary to Enniscorthy she made us draw a map and mark on it where Enniscorthy was, to state in the margin what its longitude and latitude were, to discover and write down its population. She told us about the Battle of Vinegar Hill, and explained that County Wexford wasn't at all like County Tipperary, being affected to this day by Viking settlements. Wexford people were called Kulchies, she said. The pronunciation of certain words in Irish would be different in County Wexford. She read us the lines of a Wexford song — Kelly the Boy from Killanne — a rousing evocation of our woeful national struggle in the south-east corner of Ireland.

Learning was never again to be as calm or as agreeable as it was in that upstairs room with Miss Quirke. Yet to come was all that disappointment in the eyes of weary schoolmasters, and text-books thrown, verbal abuse, physical attack. Miss Quirke just taught.

Mary Quirke she was. A Christmas card came, with holly drawn just as she had demonstrated, berries dotted in with modest panache. Was she no more than seventeen when she rode in every day from Oola? Was she in love with the man with the moustache when she paused to fill the basket of her bicycle with sprigs from the hedges? Again her Relief nib dips into the bottle of Stephens' red ink, again her soft voice forgives yet another foolish mistake. Did ever she come to know the Champs-Élysées, or did she simply slip back into the County Tipperary landscape? Of all the people I have ever known, Miss Quirke deserved the Champs-Élysées.

(1992)

Bad Trip

THERE HAVE BEEN terrible, ugly journeys that are remembered by me now for different aspects of distress. Races against time have been lost. Delays at airports have triumphantly ruined weekends. Night has come down too soon when walking in the Alps. Theft has brought travel to a halt, toothache made a nightmare of it. Once a ferry mistakenly took off before its passengers had arrived on the quayside. Once the wheels of an aircraft did not come down. '*Kaputt!*' a German garage mechanic declared of an old A.30 on an autobahn, and that was that.

But the worst journey of my life involved neither hardship, pain nor danger. It was not particularly uncomfortable. I suffered neither undue hunger nor thirst, extremes of neither heat nor cold. What possessed me was dread, and the misery of anticipating the unavoidable.

I was twelve years old on the morning of 28 April 1941, returning to boarding-school by bus, from the town of Enniscorthy in the south-east corner of Ireland, to Dublin. Some time the previous January I had made this journey for the first time. I had waited with my brother outside the paper-shop where the bus drew in at the bottom of Slaney Hill. Our two trunks and our bicycles were on the pavement; other members of the family had come to wave good-bye. Too excited to say anything, we had watched the red and cream-coloured bus approaching on the other side of the river, crossing the bridge, then slowing down. We had egg sandwiches and Toblerone. Our spirits were high.

On this second occasion I was alone because my brother was ill. Otherwise everything was apparently the same. People had come to wave good-bye, bicycle and trunk were hoisted on to the roof of the bus and secured beneath a tarpaulin. A washbag and anything else necessary for the night was packed into a small suitcase known at the school as a pyjama suitcase. But everything was different also, dogged by a grim

29

unease that the thirteen weeks following that first occasion had inspired. Journey to hell, I said to myself as the conductor handed me my ticket and my change. 'How're you doing?' he enquired, red-faced and cheery. Bleakly, I told him I was all right.

By the time we reached Bunclody the odour of long-boiled cabbage that hung about the school's kitchen and dining-room was beginning to mingle with the bus's exhaust fumes. By Kildavin, the noise of the play-yard echoed; by Tullow, Monsieur Bertain was striking the blackboard in a fury. In Rathvilly the sarcastic science master was in full flow.

An old man had halted the bus at Ballycarney crossroads and now sat beside me, shredding a plug of tobacco. He wore a cap and a rough grey suit, neither collar nor tie. He had entered the bus with a brown-paper parcel under his arm, greeting everyone as he made his way along the aisle. He was travelling to Dublin to see his daughter, who'd just been taken into hospital. He whispered hoarsely, telling me this. The parcel contained a nightdress he'd borrowed from a neighbour. 'She sent me a wire to bring a nightdress,' he said.

When my brother and I made the first journey to school our delight had increased with every mile. There would be dormitories, we had been told; games we'd only heard about — cricket and rugby — would be played. A shopman in Enniscorthy who had been at this school assured us that we'd love it, since he had loved it himself. We imagined the playing fields, and the day boys arriving on their bicycles every morning, the boarders companionably going for walks at the week-ends. Going for walks, and visits to the Museum and the Zoo, were mentioned in the prospectus. So was the excellence of the food, atten-tion paid to health and well-being, the home-from-home atmosphere. The motherliness of the housekeeper was not mentioned, but we'd heard about it from the shopman. He said the masters were a decent lot.

'You're off for the two days?' The old man had coaxed his pipe to smoulder to his satisfaction and was emitting billows of acrid smoke. He didn't listen when I told him I was going back to school, but continued about his daughter being admitted to hospital. A worse misfortune had occurred in the past, when she'd married a Dublin man.

'He has her short of garment money,' the old man said. 'That's why she sent the wire.' His daughter had two broken legs. She'd been on the roof of a hen-shed when it gave way. He crossed himself. She was lucky she hadn't been killed.

It was a sunny day. The side of my face next to the window was warm. Cows rested in the fields we passed, not even chewing their cuds. A few stood on a riverbank, drooping over it, too lazy to drink. Primroses were in bloom.

'Plenty more for anyone!' The stern voice of the motherly house-keeper echoed, as the other voices had. In the middle of each morning the entire school congregated in the kitchen passage and received a bakelite tumblerful of soup. It was a yellowish colour, with globules of grease floating on the surface. Chunks of potato and turnip sank to the bottom, and an excess of barley made the mixture difficult to consume: you had to open your mouth as wide as you could and tip the tumbler into it, feeling sick while you did so.

'A right gurrier,' the old man said. His daughter's husband had ordered her up on the roof to repair it. 'Roasting himself at the range while she's risking her limbs on old corrugated iron. A lead-swinger from Tallagh. Useless.'

We'd have giggled, my brother and I. We'd have listened to all that with pleasure if we'd heard it on our first journey to school. We'd have egged the old man on.

'Dooley's coming up!' the conductor called out. 'Anyone for Dooley's?'

The early morning, when you first woke up, was the worst. You lay there listening to the noises coming from the three other beds — someone muttering in his sleep, someone softly snoring, the bedsprings creaking when there was a sudden movement. There were no curtains on the windows. The light of dawn brought silhouettes first, and then the reality of the room: the fawn top blankets, the boarded-up fireplace. You didn't want to go back to sleep because if you did you'd have to wake up again. 'Get out of that bed,' the Senior Boarder ordered when the bell went. 'Out at the double, pull the bedclothes back. Quick now!' He glared from the sheets, his acned features ugly on the pillow. He was said to pray before he rose.

'Isn't that a grand day?' a woman shouted into the bus when it drew in at Dooley's, a wayside public house. She pushed a parcel in and the conductor ambled down to collect it. A grand day, he agreed. When the bus moved on, the woman stood there, waving after it, smiling

in the sunlight. *Guinness is Good for You*, the sign in the public-house window said. A sweeping-brush stood in the open doorway, propped against the door-frame. Tulips grew in a tin bath that had been painted green.

The Upper Fifth bully used to pretend he was going to brand you. He'd put a poker in the open fire in the Fourth Form and two of his butties would hold your arms and legs, a third guarding the door. When the poker was red-hot it would be held close to your cheek and you could feel the heat. 'Don't blub,' the one with the poker warned. 'You'll get it if you blub.' The sarcastic science master was a one-time amateur boxer, known in ringside circles as the Battling Bottlebrush, something to do with the effect of the aggressive instinct on his hair. It was sleeked back now with brilliantine, as tidy as the rest of him.

He lived with his mother, and was said to be as gentle as a lamb with her.

The Irish and Geometry master lived in the school itself, in an attic room festooned with the rugby togs he pegged out to air. He was a tall, brisk, brown-suited man with a narrow brown moustache. He played rugby for Wanderers and often on a Saturday afternoon we went to Lansdowne Road to watch him, hungry-looking on the wing. Otherwise he was more heard than seen, the melancholy playing of a violin drifting down the uncarpeted attic stairs or through his open window. The masters were said to be ill-paid.

'Two broken legs.' The old man had twisted himself round to address the woman in the seat behind.

'God help her,' the woman sympathised.

In the dormitory Corrigan would tell us about his adventures with the maid. After lights-out his voice would drone on, no one believing a word he said. Little Vincent from Limerick would snuffle into the bedclothes. 'Shut up that bloody filth, Corrigan!' the Senior Boarder would finally shout. His minion and his pal came from Moate and had blackheads all over his back, which he'd sometimes ask you to squeeze out for him. The Senior Boarder told you to get on with it.

On the bus I closed my eyes. It might crash, and I might be taken to a hospital like the old man's daughter, instead of having to continue the journey, on my bicycle, out to the suburb where the school was. 'Don't be a child,' the Senior Boarder had a way of saying if you said you couldn't eat something or if you didn't want to play the boarders' game of catching a tennis-ball when it rolled off the roofs of the outhouses, wet and dirty from the gutter water.

'That's shocking altogether,' the woman behind me indignantly exclaimed. 'She could've been lying there dead.'

If the bus crashed there might be instant blackness, and you'd be lying there dead yourself. You wouldn't know a thing about it. You'd be buried in the graveyard by the church, and everyone would be sorry that you'd been made to go on this fateful journey. Little Vincent would snuffle all night when he heard the news. 'Don't be a child,' the Senior Boarder would snap at him.

The bus stopped in Baltinglass and I thought I'd maybe get out. I imagined slipping away and nobody noticing, my bicycle and trunk still under the tarpaulin, carried on to Dublin. I imagined walking through the fields, warmed by the sun, not caring what happened next.

'Did you ever hear the like of it?' the old man asked me. 'No more than twenty-five years of age she is.'

I shook my head. I said I never had. At breakfast there were doorsteps of fried bread, one for each boarder, not crispy, as fried bread was at home, but sodden and floppy with fat. The Senior Boarder poured out tea that tasted of metal. 'What's this?' the housekeeper sniffily demanded, examining your darned pullover. She'd never seen worse darning, she declared, and you remembered your mother threading wool through a needle and then carefully beginning the small repair.

The bus arrived at the first straggle of Dublin's outskirts, then pressed relentlessly on through Templeogue and Terenure and into the city proper. When it finally drew up on Aston Quay it felt for the first time like a friend, its smoky, hot interior a refuge I had never valued. 'Are you right there, son?' The cheery conductor wagged his head at me.

On the street I strapped the pyjama suitcase on to the carrier of my bicycle. I dawdled over that; I watched the old man who'd sat beside me crossing the street, the brown-paper parcel containing his daughter's nightdress under his arm. Other passengers from the bus were moving away also. I mounted my bicycle, a Golden Eagle, and rode into the traffic of Westmoreland Street. The trunk would be delivered to the school later, with all the other trunks.

Arrival is an end, the journey over, a destination reached. That is usually so, but on this occasion journey and destination were one; this time there was no sigh of gratitude from the weary traveller, no long-earned moment of relief. My Golden Eagle carried me only to a realm in which the highways and byways were sealed against escape, a part of hell in which everyone was someone else's victim.

Irrelevantly, trams clanked by. Crowds bustled on the pavements. 'How delightful to see you again!' the science master sneered already, and the Senior Boarder drove his elbow into a passing stomach. There would be fresh adventures with the maid, more out-of-reach blackheads. Mechanically, as though I had no will, my feet worked the pedals. When a red light demanded it, I applied the brakes, obedient in all things. Already I could hear the Irish master's violin. I could taste the yellow soup.

I turned out of Harcourt Street into Charlemont Street and later crossed the Grand Canal. My egg sandwiches and Toblerone remained uneaten. The chocolate would have melted into my pyjamas and washbag: dully, it passed through my mind that the motherly house-keeper would have an excuse to say something harsh almost as soon as she saw me. Slowly, I turned into the short avenue that led to the school. I rode past the carpentry hut and pushed the Golden Eagle into the bicycle shed. I walked through the play-yard, continuing the endless journey.

(1989)

The Bull

'A.D. CORDONER WAS the headmaster of Sandford Park in Dublin, otherwise known as the Bull because he had once roared like one at Boland's older brother. Majestic in a blue suit, he was a man of considerable passion, the greater part of which lay in his love of cricket. He had two subsidiary obsessions, one for spelling-bees and the other for whistling the 'British Grenadiers'. The great nuisances in his life were the Sandford Cinema and men in semi-clerical dress who attempted to get into conversation with his boys, with the bespectacled Warren in particular. He had no scholastic qualifications of any kind. Once upon a time he'd played cricket for the Gentlemen of Ireland.

Massively, the Bull would surge through the boarding-house with the 'British Grenadiers' in full throat, and all eleven boarders would rise and remain standing until he passed on. If he forgot to take the roll at morning assembly — which as far as we could see was his only daily task — he would later appear in the various classrooms to tick off the names in his vast roll-book.

A monumental innocence, matching his physical bulk, ruled this man. He belonged to a G.A. Henty world in which the game was always played according to time-honoured gentlemen's rules, in which no one was unmanly or ignoble. The thieving of text-books was rife at the school, Durell and Fawdrys, and Longman's Latin primers disappearing by the dozen to the city's secondhand bookshops. A.D. Cordoner never knew a thing about it. At night the boarders slipped out into Ranelagh to buy fish and chips. Local apple trees were stripped. There were liaisons with the girls from the convent. He wouldn't have believed it.

'Where's Truman?' he would enquire if he drew a blank when he called his roll, and he often did with this particular name. 'Anyone know where friend Truman is today?' Those of us who were boarders jealously imagined friend Truman hanging about O'Connell Street, waiting for the cinemas to open. Truman was a wit, the funniest boy in the school. He could draw Veronica Lake's profile and emit saliva in a mist. He could imitate his mother's handwriting. He rolled his trousers up and crouched at the box-office of the Carlton or the Metropole, hoping to persuade the cashier that he was under fourteen. He was clever, red-haired and different, and did as little work as possible. Answering an instinct that was otherwise dormant, the Bull didn't trust him. 'I see you about the place with Truman,' he accused me once, but he said no more, leaving me with the impression that some conclusion, or warning, eluded him.

In conversation with the Bull you had a feeling that he didn't know things because he somehow wasn't meant to, that he didn't make certain statements because their implications were alien to him. The men in semi-clerical dress had been forced upon him because the sluggish Warren, in his tightly-belted navy-blue mackintosh, repeatedly became involved with them on his way to and from the shop where he bought the model aeroplane kits he never completed. When Warren was approached for the third or fourth time we explained to him that all you had to do was to tell the men to go away. Protectively, we added that there was no point in bothering the Bull with stuff like that. But Warren derived a degree of personal glory from his retailing of these encounters and on each occasion the Bull was obliged — no doubt in extreme embarrassment — to telephone the Guards.

The Sandford Cinema, next door to the school, was an irritant simply because it was there. 'Are you sure?' the Bull would enquire every Saturday evening when a boarders' delegation designated whatever film was showing as one of educational interest. 'Is it known to be good? What's it called, laddies?' In his sombre, bachelor study *They Died With their Boots on*, *Broadway Melody of 1940* and many others became classics of the cinema, and every Saturday he said he supposed we knew what we were talking about. He was at a disadvantage, having never, himself, seen a film of any kind.

His study, on the ground floor, the door always closed, was his sanctuary. All his meals were taken there, carried to him on a tray three times a day. In an uncomfortable leather armchair drawn up close to the fire he read the Sexton Blake paperbacks he found lying about the boarders' lounge. Governors' meetings took place in the study, and governors' dinners; boys were upbraided there, would-be parents offered tea and wafer biscuits. The school dining-room was in

the basement, between the evil-smelling kitchen and the bedroom the
maids shared. The Bull never descended those stairs. He rarely left the
study except to go to bed or to conduct a spelling-bee, to mark the
roll-book or stroll about the cricket pitch. Sometimes on Sundays he
led the boarders to Sandford church, sometimes he chose not to, and
we went on our own. People said he had a sister with whom he spent
the holidays, but if he had we never saw her. Certainly there was no
wife, and it was impossible to imagine that there ever might have been.

The casual nature of my previous education — the repeated changing
of schools, longish periods when no school at all was attended —
combined with various personal ineptitudes to leave me backward
in all subjects except English, and algebra, for which I possessed an
odd percipience. When I failed to perform adequately in the Bull's
spelling-bees he said it didn't matter. 'Fuchsia?' he would say when he
came across me. 'Sorghum?' I asked him what sorghum was once and
he said that didn't matter either.

When I was new I could tell from his interested scrutiny that he
was wondering if I'd be any good at cricket. 'Well done, laddie,' he
said, taking it as a sign when I managed to get a place in the under-14
rugby side. On raw spring evenings all the boarders would walk with
him around the playing field, until we came at last to the sacred, fenced-
off strip. The Bull would rub his huge hands slowly together and say
it was greening nicely. Then we'd walk back to the school. 'Potamic?'
the rest of the conversation would go. 'Sanderling?'

When summer came I disappointed him. The art of protecting three
stumps from a hard ball travelling at speed was something I knew from
the start I had no chance of mastering. Stranded at the wicket, I felt it
to be a dangerous, tedious game. When you were fielding there were
boys behind you practising in the nets, driving balls with considerable
force toward the back of your head. I didn't at all care for that.

But from two o'clock on Saturdays, after the day boys had gone
home, the Bull had his eleven boarders on the pitch for five hours
at a stretch. And on Sundays we'd be at it again. You could never
escape on Saturdays and Sundays, and on weekdays when it was fine
the Bull would announce that he wanted every single boy in whites that
afternoon, either playing or practising in the nets. Even boys who for
medical reasons were not permitted to play should change into whites,
and sit and watch. His benign eye became stern as it sought out Truman,

a clear signal that during the course of the afternoon it would several times seek him out again.

But if the Bull didn't suspect you might abscond he didn't keep you particularly in his sights. Once seen, you could take a chance, slipping over the wall behind the shrubbery, into the yard the Sandford Sweeteries shared with the cinema. By poking at the automatic locking device you could get in through one of the exit doors, or failing that through the window of the Ladies. I saw *The Fleet's In* on a cricketing afternoon, and *The Stars Look Down* and *Crash Dive*, all of them accompanied by news reels and Leon Errol or Charlie Chase shorts. Another attractive way of passing these sunny afternoons was to meet the girls from the convent. We sat with them on the banks of the Dodder, eating jamroll you could buy at half price after four o'clock in one of the Ranelagh bakeries, occasionally sharing a cigarette. The girls were quite taken with our whites.

I left Sandford Park when a new Latin master turned out to be a man who'd been the headmaster of the notorious Tate School in Wexford, which I had once attended for six weeks. 'I understand you were removed after a dispute,' was how the Bull rather nervously put it, handing me a letter from my father which contained an ultimatum: if the newly-appointed Latin master remained I would not. Not wishing to sustain the loss of a boarding fee, the Bull sought my support. 'Do what you can, laddie,' he begged, sending me home for a long weekend on the grounds that it was half-term.

I failed him. Having become used to surroundings I had once dreaded, I argued the Bull's case for him, but to no avail. Still backward in all subjects except English and algebra, I was taken away.

Years later I was told about the death of the Bull, in his bed in the middle of the night. The boarders rallied round, looking after him in death as they had in life, surprised by the sense of deprivation they experienced. He wasn't one of the world's great headmasters; indeed he was hardly a headmaster at all. He was a child among adults, even if the adults were sometimes no more than eight years of age. But his naïvety was a great deal more refreshing than those qualities of leadership and purpose more ordinarily associated with his profession. He did no harm. No one was frightened when he roared.

(1973)

The Warden's Wife

A T NIGHT THE lights of Dublin blinked below us, away from us
to the sea. On a clear day, from halfway up Kilmashogue, you
could see across to Wales. St Columba's, with a reputation for aloofness,
and skill on the hockey field, is set high in the Dublin mountains, established there in the 1840s by the Victorian cleric who was later to found
Radley. 'Be ye as wise as serpents and as gentle as doves' had been the
saint's catchphrase, as many a sermon reminded us.

St Columba's is the only public school of its kind in the Republic of
Ireland, small within a small minority yet with a certain *cachet*, more
confident of itself now than once it was. 'That this House believes we
are an outpost of empire' was a debating motion the term I arrived
there for the last two years of my fragmentary education, knowing
little of such delicate areas of life as art and music, the theatre and
literature. My provincial accent was noticeable and was mocked. The
rougher ambience of recent boarding establishments had not prepared
me for the fact that pretty junior boys were called *bijous*, and that the
poet Horace — laboured through with the assistance of Dr Giles's Keys
to the Classics — was more interesting because of that. In all sorts of
ways it was at St Columba's where I first became aware that black and
white are densities of more complicated greys.

Gowns were worn in the classroom and in Dining Hall, and surplices
in Chapel on Sundays. The gowns covered the top half of the body
only, and somewhat inadequately, but were useful for smuggling slices
of bread to toast in the furnace room, for soaking up spills and polishing
shoes. Traditionally, no junior was permitted to walk about with his
hands in his pockets. Traditionally on St Patrick's Day the entire school,
even the stout housekeeper, the cook, the bursar's secretary and the two
school nurses, assisted in the planting of potatoes. Traditionally, there
were cock-fights — one boy perched on another's shoulders, lashing

out at a pair of rivals — and Cloister Cricket, and words with local meanings, different from the accepted ones, and small idiosyncracies of behaviour. Traditionally, the first fruits of the potato-planting were eaten on St Columba's Day.

In a sprawling deerpark there was a ruined summer-house where Robert Emmet was said to have courted Sarah Curran. There was a butler — a melancholy man called Flood, said to be the only survivor of a torpedoed troopship in the First World War — and a vast number of maids, the most memorable of whom was a lanky bespectacled girl known as the Bicycle. There was a Mr Chips — sweet-tempered and white-haired — from whose tobacco pouch you might occasionally take a fill, but were on guard when he hove into sight in the Junior Dormitory on the occasions when some minor ailment sent you to bed early. There were variations of Mr Perrin's relationship with Mr Trail. The headmaster was known as the Warden.

In spite of its crème-de-la-crème reputation, St Columba's in 1944 was a genuine microcosm. You didn't have to be clever to be there; and the sons of shopkeepers rubbed shoulders with the sons of farmers, bank officials, hard-nosed Northern businessmen, and aristocrats of the old Ascendancy. Reduced fees saw clergymen's sons through; well-to-do relatives were called upon by the impecunious. When it chose to, the school became a world of its own. Double-saving time was kept one summer, clocks an hour ahead of standard Irish time. No bathing attire was ever worn in the hilltop swimming-pool, by boys or masters, since no one ever passed by. The school's meat was slaughtered on the premises; its farm supplied all vegetables and milk.

*

On the periphery was the Warden's wife. So shy that communication often seemed excruciating for her, the headmaster's wife was a bent figure in her forties, fingers tightly interlocked behind her back when she crept, crablike, into Dining Hall or Chapel. Her clothes were drab. Stockings of coarse blue wool established for her — though hardly by design — a certain intellectual reputation. Grey hair bushed horizontally from either side of her head, and the effort of smiling was clearly not easy. It was difficult to think up something to say to her.

Her husband was small and red-skinned, especially about the face, round and bouncy, like a ball. He was an English clergyman with a

Home Counties accent, given to repeating that the Chapel was the centre of school life. He regularly drew attention to a metal pouch, which he kept beneath glass, declaring that it had once contained the holy writings of St Columba. He spoke frequently about a cow that was being fattened on the farm for dispatch to one of the ravaged areas of Europe as soon as hostilities ceased. 'Nellie the Post-War Cow,' he jollily called this animal, the extra syllable he introduced into the word 'cow' a joy for mimics. Our diet was an enviable one, we were regularly informed, and heard details of its calorific value. Bromide was added, we believed.

The Warden's wife was invariably silent while this inconsequential chatter was pursued. Her eyes were of some dark hue, not notably blue or brown, possibly black. Once she had been beautiful: I often heard that said during my two years at St Columba's and perhaps it was true. Perhaps photographs had been seen, or perhaps it was that since she appeared to have no present she was being given a past. Gossip abhors a vacuum: in schools it is often without foundation, spun to break monotony. All that was certain was that no beauty remained.

Obliged to play some social part in her husband's ambitions for the school, she played no part whatsoever in its day-to-day routine. She was there at the lunchtime High Table, when the Warden was joined by his prefects, and at Sunday breakfast, when he was joined by his staff. On Sunday evenings she appeared in Chapel. Otherwise, her life was private. She weeded flowerbeds in that part of the garden forbidden to the boys; only glimpses were caught of her, a shadow skulking by.

Born Mary Savery in 1901 — as I later discovered — she went to school in Ealing, attended both Oxford and Cambridge, obtaining a First in Theology at Lady Margaret Hall, the second woman to do so. Her awkwardness might have passed unnoticed in higher academic life, but could not in a community of beady-eyed boys. No one ever commented that this was an extraordinary marriage, yet in retrospect it seems like that. She was an intelligent woman, her husband a figure of fun. Yet the curate she'd been drawn to at Oxford may have given no hint of how the years would shape him later: pomposity does not always flower early, and the blinkers of those who court power are acquired as the power itself is.

'Bad taste' was the Warden's favourite expression when we knew him: in his clipped Cockney tones he railed against it as he might against the Devil Incarnate. He dropped so many names, and so frequently referred to his entry in *Who's Who*, that this coinage in his conversation had become as debased as his references to the post-war cow. Athletics had been his sport; honouring this healthy pursuit, he led the school on a misty afternoon run through the deerpark to the mountains beyond it. The mist became rain, and when a short-cut was considered wise there was an unhappy encounter with a local farmer. 'Get off my land, you red-faced Saxon!' roared this man, to the delight of a hundred and sixty boys.

We never wondered what she made of it. We listened when her husband reported, personally, the nature of RAF successes over Germany and the number of Luftwaffe planes destroyed. Did she, as many of us did, question the flattening of Dresden and the slaughter of its people at a time when the war was almost over and no military targets were involved? If she did, no doubt it was done silently.

Every so often the gaunt, cassocked figure of Brother Charles — a roving confessor — arrived to ease the guilt of persistent sinners. Repenting suicide attempts and thefts from the collection plate in Chapel, or practices culled from the *Encyclopaedia of Sex*, became a game, its culmination to catch Brother Charles's eye when later in the Warden's company. How often from her solitude must she have noticed what we were up to? How often must she have caught the whisper of a giggle when her husband, yet again, drew attention to the watercolour he claimed to be by Turner or the chest he insisted had been the property of Anne Boleyn?

There were three children of the headmaster's marriage, two girls and a boy. Rosemary was the older of the girls, a pert adolescent with a small army of followers from the middle and senior schools. Perhaps for want of anything better to report, gossip suggested that the Warden's wife took more than a passing interest in her older daughter's conquests. Tongue-tied among her husband's prefects at the lunchtime High Table, she was quoted as having once referred, out of the blue, to breast-feeding. So the rumour began that beneath an unprepossessing exterior, and perhaps related to her beauty in the past, this woman was more than a little aware of sex, her reference to her breasts as much evidence of it as her interest in 'what went on' between her daughter and her followers. That she was allied to a man who was the declared enemy of the sensual life in all its aspects struck none of us as tragedy.

*

Late in my career at St Columba's I was involved in a series of late-night excursions to a grill-room in the centre of Dublin. We roused one another at half-past twelve or one, crept from our dormitories, and borrowed the first bicycles that came to hand in the bicycle sheds. It was eight miles, all downhill, to the Green Rooster in O'Connell Street, where we ordered plates of fried food. Afterwards, rousing the night porter at the Shelbourne Hotel, we attempted, always unsuccessfully, to persuade him to supply us with drink. The next day we made up for our loss of sleep during Maurie Wigham's ineffably tedious double period of biology. Maurie Wigham was always relieved to see boys asleep because the level of noise was less.

On the afternoon of 8 May 1945, the school and staff were summoned and the Warden announced that the war in Europe was over. He gave us details. He read out statements made by the German generals, and by Winston Churchill. It was, he said, a great day for the world and for the school, and added that he wished to see immediately all boys who had been breaking school rules by cycling down to Dublin in the middle of the night. It was suspected that he had known for some time but had held his fire, aware that the end of the war was close and might well be an occasion for spirited celebration.

Because it was one of the few nightspots in Dublin at that time, the Green Rooster was popularly rumoured to be a house of ill repute. With the interest in sexual matters ascribed to her, the Warden's wife was said to have alerted her husband to our true purpose in visiting it since he, in his reluctance even to consider that sensual desire could occur in adolescence, would naturally not have suspected this. In spite of the fact that the Green Rooster was innocent of its racy reputation, random expulsions immediately took place and in one case there was talk of legal action against the school for defamation of character.

If the Warden's wife had a rôle in the affair, it had probably to do more with an awareness of the world than with the nature of carnality. On the only occasion she spoke more than a few words to me in private it was to ascertain the truth or falsity of something that clearly interested her a great deal more than this imputed obsession. A boy was conducting an experiment with his digestion by not eating.

'Is this so?' the Warden's wife enquired, interrupting the pruning of a rose, secateurs still poised.

45

'Yes,' I said.

'How long?'

'More than a fortnight now. That's what they say.'

'Nothing at all?'

'He allows himself tea and milk.'

'And why is he doing this? Is he protesting in some way?'

'He's interested in a medical sense.'

'Has he discovered anything? Is there a noticeable difference in him?'

'His breath is bad.'

She nodded. It would be so, she agreed, only adding as she returned to her roses that some of the saints who starved themselves must have developed unpleasant breath; their cells or caves could not have been agreeable places to visit. I went away, feeling I shared a secret with her, for I was certain that the conversation we had had would not be confided to her husband. It would not fascinate him, as clearly it had fascinated her, that a boy was experimenting with starvation. It was enough that there were communists among his charges, and those who would not bow their heads during the Creed. He took them to task, exacting promises that satisfied him. He set his store by the sensible, the conforming, the moderate and the clean of mind.

'Why?' he asked when I refused to become a prefect.

'I belong in the ranks, sir.'

A blue bulb lit up outside the study door when he did not wish to be disturbed. He reached out for the connecting switch. He told me to sit down.

'That's where my friends are, sir.'

'Ah.'

Behind his desk, he leaned back, rounder and redder than ever. He examined me steadily and then spoke very rapidly, telling me about his early days at Keble College, Oxford, and about a friend of his, another headmaster, who slept at nights with three volumes on his bedside table: the Bible, *Alice in Wonderland* and *The Lighter Side of School Life* by Ian Hay. He spoke particularly of the latter and it was, in fact, *The Lighter Side of School Life* by Ian Hay with which I left the study.

Later I agreed to become a prefect because it was easier to say yes. It became my privilege to sit at the end of a table in Dining Hall for breakfast and tea, to refuse all food at those meals if I wished, to swagger a bit. Small boys acted as my servants, washing the dishes

46

from which I had eaten eggs or baked beans in the common room. At High Table lunch the prefects moved one seat to the left each day, so that once every so often a meal was taken next to the Warden and the following day next to his wife. I remember nothing of the Warden's conversation on these occasions except his once divulging that he preferred waxy to floury potatoes. I recall his being encouraged to expand on the preference, to name the potatoes referred to, the subject then advanced so that we might hear his opinion of mashed potatoes, roast, fried and chipped potatoes, and which varieties were most suitable for each form of cooking. Sniggering was stifled. Flood the butler helped himself to a morsel of meat, which he often did when tedium set in.

Next to the Warden's wife, you had to bend your head in her direction because sometimes she was hard to hear. This was no doubt so when she had made her famous reference to breast-feeding. 'You should go and see *Ill Met by Moonlight*,' she advised me, referring to a play by Micheál MacLiammóir. The next time round she suggested a visit to O'Casey's *Red Roses for Me*. Since I was the editor of the school magazine, she asked me if I intended to become a journalist and advised me that if I ever did I should first become an expert on a particular subject, and corner it. 'I don't know what', she murmured, softly, 'I would have chosen to know a lot about.' But something in her tone suggested that she did.

'A veterinary surgeon, is it?' her husband speculated when my schooldays ended. 'You're becoming a vet?'

'No, sir.'

'Ah. Now why did I imagine you were to be a vet?'

'I'm afraid I don't know, sir.'

'Nor I. Nor I. You're sure about this?'

'I think you're confusing me with Gahan, sir.'

'Nonsense. I know full well who you are.'

The end of every term was rich in ceremony. All library books were handed back a week or so in advance so that stocks might be checked, so that no one could wander off with the Phaidon edition of Frans Hals or *Brave New World*. There was a considerable to-do about the organisation of laundry, and trunks were fetched from the luggage room. The school photograph, taken a fortnight before, was attached to a board outside Dining Hall.

'Ah yes, I'd meant to mention that. You look grumpy in the photograph.'

'I'm sorry, sir. It's just my usual —'

'Prefects should set a less cheerless example. On occasion we all have to smile, you know, whether we like it or not.'

'I understand, sir.'

'You'll find in life that a happy disposition is half the battle. And in your chosen vocation you'll find that a smile does not come amiss with a dumb beast. I would warn you against the affectation of melancholy.'

'Yes, sir.'

'God's way is cheerfulness.'

'I see, sir.'

'I am glad that you do. A grumpy countenance achieves nothing.'

'No, sir.'

'I note you were not present when the conjuror visited recently. In that respect I would warn you against intellectual arrogance. Turn over a new leaf. In the beautiful words of the hymn, go smiling forth yet humility know.'

'I will of course, sir.'

On the last night of term I joined the trail of boys who lined up to shake the masters' hands, many of them bidding a final farewell. Afterwards there was tea in the drawing-room for the prefects. The Warden's wife was in a corner, no one bothering her, which no doubt was what she wished. More than ever, she looked the victim of her circumstances. Roaring boys had invented a life for her, pressing her uneasily into adolescent fantasy. She did not belong there: she occupied a twilight of her own. She bowed before the brash cockiness of a clergyman who resembled a ball; for all her years in this place only her blue stockings had caught the eye as she crept meekly through the shadows cast by pedagogues. Did she, as she pondered in her flower-beds, shuffle through her regrets, or wish she had her life over again? For a moment I wanted to say good-bye to her before hurrying off to celebrate the end of school in some more suitable way. But I was shy and didn't.

*

Forty-three years went by and there, in the *Old Columban*, was her obituary. She died on 5 July 1989 in Toronto, to which city she had dutifully accompanied her husband, again to be a headmaster's wife. Describing her as a 'sad and lonely woman', her obituarist revealed a

48

single startling fact. During her years in the Dublin mountains she had become expert on matters pertaining to the turf, regularly attending race-meetings.

No one had ever said the Warden's wife was good for a tip; no one had ever imagined her laying an on-course bet. She did not seek inside information from Cog Chapman, whose father had a stables. She did not speak of Gordon Richards or Charlie Smirke; nor Kinsale Girl at Punchestown, nor Golden Miller in his heyday. Yet this woman, who on the face of it had been smudged away to nothing, dwelt profitably on form among the callous prefects at High Table lunches, while her husband held forth about potatoes or recalled the day he met de Valera.

Forty-three years on, there is a woman who, obedient to the code of the times, never revealed her feelings about the humbug of so much that surrounded her, a woman who is bored by married life and family life and the petty world of school, who is more mysterious than anyone had ever guessed. Grandstands and bets, bookies and tick-tack men, mocked the paucity of our invention. Had she gone alone, even secretly, to race-meetings? The pursed moral tone of her husband would hardly have permitted his habitual presence. Had she laughed silently at all of us? Would she have liked to be a racing-page seer, a Captain Crack or Your Old Reliable?

A finger, now, runs down a list of runners; a note is pencilled, chances weighed. *Next time out, Lovely Cottage. Rip Van Winkle, surely pulled? Persian Gulf for a place.*

'Plagues on you according to your sins,' warns the Senior Prefect in Chapel, smug as an old man. *Caughoo could do it if the going's soft*. In the drawing-room, yet again, comes the information about Anne Boleyn's chest; attention is drawn to the watercolour by Turner. Tea is poured and sponge cake cut, the teacups passed about. Deaf in her solitude, the Warden's wife muses among gaudy silks enriched with hoops and diamonds, half-moons and stars. Held-back wagers are placed, trainers offer a final word, and then the old-faced jockeys leap sprightly to the saddle. In the drawing-room the precious metal pouch is declared once more to have been the repository of holy writings. In the drawing-room there is the thunder of hooves.

(1992)

Mentors

I COULDN'T, I protested. I wasn't deft with my hands. I couldn't
even draw.

'Oh, just get on with it,' Kelly, an exasperated art master, ordered.
'Just do it, for God's sake!'

And I did it because at least it would be a change from traipsing over
the hillsides in search of a rock or a clump of gorse to sketch, or going
to see what the ram was up to. What I had agreed to do instead was to
carve an eagle in low relief. Anyone could, Kelly impatiently insisted.

He was wrong. If the chisel wasn't sharp enough it tore at the
wood, leaving it shredded and hairy. Sharpening the chisel was a
knack, and carving with it was a knack. The more you hacked, the
less the carefully pencilled outline resembled a proud bird of prey.
Perspective disappeared. If you didn't clamp the wood firmly enough
it slipped about, resisting all attentions; if you tightened the clamps they
left an ugly indentation. If you dealt the chisel too powerful a blow with
the trickily rounded mallet the eagle's claws weren't there any more. If
you didn't look after your fingers they wouldn't be there either. Most
of the time there was blood all over the place.

But there was something about the arduous, unsatisfactory activity
that was appealing. When a delicate little gauge was as sharp as a razor
it slipped pleasurably through the grain of the wood, and for an instant
or two you could control it perfectly. The grain was a pattern to make
use of, a means of suggesting concavity or depth, an emphasis when you
wanted it to be. In time — five or six weeks — I finished the eagle and
Kelly advised me simply to polish it with beeswax, but I chose instead
to plaster on raw linseed oil, which had the effect of bringing out all
the flaws. Kelly said I'd ruined it.

A Place for Everything and Everything in its Place was inscribed on
the art-room wall, Kelly being a tidy, matter-of-fact man. Pill Kelly

he was known as, a way of intimating that he was not as popular as his flamboyant predecessor had been. He didn't have a beard then, and he signed his watercolours *Austen Kelly*. But in the autumn of that year he ceased to shave and changed his Christian name to Oisín. As well as art, he taught French and Irish, and was generally considered to be well below average at conveying the rudiments of both. He was, as he often said himself, in it for the money.

In the art room he didn't fulsomely encourage. His example of doing rather than thinking, his dislike of the amateur, his distrust of philosophy, of the cerebral and the academic, weren't thrust upon you: they were there, you shared them or you didn't, you stood on your own two feet. He was impatient and tetchy and down-to-earth. You weren't put into the world to be pampered. If you wanted to learn, listen to what was being said to you; if you didn't, no one else was going to fret.

Kelly would ride about the place on a fat old farmhorse, seeming happy up there, far removed from the rudiments of French and Irish. In the art room he offered short-cuts, tricks of the trade, skills that could be acquired. Art itself, he knew without ever saying it, could not be taught. He was angered by charm and mess, and sometimes pondered on his own prickliness in this respect. 'I should go into a pub more often,' he used to say. 'Maybe pick up a few social graces.' But he couldn't be bothered with the chattery life; he hated wasting time and any kind of palaver; he was a man of the people. 'Find yourself a set of chisels,' he grumbled when carving became an obsession with me. 'You can't go on blunting mine.'

I found them in Enniscorthy, the property of an elderly woman who didn't use them any more, their boxwood handles unaffected by years of impact in the past. Kelly admired them, as he did anything of quality. 'My God!' his keen response was when the headmaster's daughter passed by the art-room window. 'Hasn't she the lovely buttocks!'

I visited Kelly on Sunday mornings in his house in Templeogue, where I would play about with chunks of clay in the conservatory he used as a studio. He sang *The Old Orange Flute* or *The Wearing of the Green* while he worked, or grumbled about the sounding of bells that controlled his daily life. The conservatory wasn't suitable for the purpose he put it to and was eventually abandoned in favour of a studio he rented in Dublin, and for which he acquired cutlery and crockery in the school dining-hall, surreptitiously slipping one article at a time under his gown at the end of each meal. 'Anyone looking?' he would enquire of the tableful of boys placed in his charge.

Oisín Kelly became one of Ireland's most distinguished sculptors, and escaped eventually from the summons of bells. Before he did so I telephoned him one day in search of some advice: my fondness for carving hadn't quietened down and I was considering becoming a professional letter-cutter. There was a silence when I mentioned advice, then came the suggestion that maybe what I wanted was information. I should have known: advice is vague, no better than opinion, not to be trusted. Information is fact, you know where you are with it. As it turned out, he gave me neither. People should make up their own minds, his reticence declared; ridiculous to ask someone else to do it for them. Stand on your own two feet; no point in possessing them otherwise.

★

R.E.C. Browne delivered a famous sermon in which he likened Christ to a Wild West sheriff, arriving to 'clean up the town'. He was the Chaplain, a big good-hearted man with a bothersome stutter, who taught English and Divinity and trained the rugby team. He bought biscuits wholesale, in huge square tins, offering them when he invited you to coffee. He was considered something of a fool.

'Come to coffee,' he would say, and you'd go because coffee was a treat and because of the biscuits. The invitation was usually issued in the evening, after prep. In summer the shadows would deepen in his study, until you couldn't see him any more and you could reach out for the biscuit tin unobserved, while he invoked Ezra Pound. '*Language is made of concrete things,*' was a favourite repetition, followed by the Pound maxim that general expressions are a laziness.

Lines from Marianne Moore, T.S. Eliot, Auden, Robert Graves, would merge in the gloom. Or there were references to accidie and concupiscence, and you didn't know if this was nonsense or not, but somehow assumed it was.

'. . . *a patient etherised upon a table,*' R.E.C. Browne would murmur at you on some other occasion, his greeting in a bustling corridor. For those he knew from the rugby field there were other greetings, and other conversations over coffee: it was said that he went in for establishing wavelengths, but we dismissed the effort, as we dismissed him too. '*The winter evening settles down,*' he would passingly declare, his stutter eased by the rhythm of the words. '*With smell of steaks in passageways.*'

One side of him was unequivocally respected: he had no difficulty in keeping order, and stood no nonsense. No one mocked him to his face, as old Daddy Evelyn — another clergyman on the staff — was mocked, or le Clerc, the geography man. With the Chaplain we trod warily without ever knowing why, and although his halting delivery was endlessly mimicked it never occurred to any of us that he was aware of the mild amusement he inadvertently provoked, and didn't care. Or that he knew the coffee and biscuits were the attraction, and didn't care either.

In retrospect all that is clearer. Adolescence is often too concerned with itself to see much beyond the boundaries of its own few years; its muddle and haste and self-protecting instinct are blinding. We saw a surface only of this Chaplain who practised public speaking with an audience of one, over coffee and biscuits. Half listened to, he tried his theories out or repeated, yet again, lines and words that nagged him.

> *Under the vapour in the fetid air*
> *Struggling with the devil of the stairs who wears*
> *The deceitful face of hope and of despair.*

As if for fun, he defined magnanimity and malice, remorse, repentance, righteousness, hypocrisy and hope. In fact, it was not for fun: twenty years later his definitions appeared as thirty-nine short articles in *A Dictionary of Christian Ethics*. Eliot and Marianne Moore, Graves and Auden, are there in his writings too. Possessor of goodness or hearty God-botherer, he found it hard simply to accept: the truth mattered most of all to him.

He passed us by, as the truth so often did too, unwelcome at that nervous time of life. Yet it was there, as hindsight shows, among his wasted definitions, lighting his perceptions of tolerance and vice, of honour, cruelty and prudence, hybris and humility. He was no prophet, he believed; but at least had seen the eternal Footman hold his coat and snicker, which is the next best thing.

He wrote to me twenty years later as to a stranger, not connecting the author of a radio play with a boy he'd once fed biscuits to. I wondered who this clergyman could be who expressed himself with such needling insight, then realised — to astonishment, dismay and shame. His voice was a vivid echo then, free of its stutter:

> *No! I am not Prince Hamlet, nor was meant to be;*
> *Am an attendant lord, one that will do*
> *To swell a progress, start a scene or two,*
> *Advise the prince; no doubt, an easy tool,*
> *Deferential, glad to be of use . . .*

★

Eccentricity when it is tediously pretended is born of a search for identity, as hell-raising often is, or a deviant stance of one kind or another. Genuine eccentrics, though, hardly know what they are, obscurely going their way in shadowy suburbs, noticed only by a few. The world they look out at is too grey for them: the peculiarities that come to govern their lives may even keep certifiable insanity at bay; often they merely fear boredom. An elderly Italian was possessed of a compulsion to live on trains irrespective of where they were going, and did so for the greater part of a long life. A Miss Gilly of Baton Rouge, Louisiana, believed it was unwise to wash the left side of the body. A Sheffield man considered it necessary to sleep with a piece of string beneath his pillow. William Ponsonby-Barker, an Ascendancy figure in nineteenth-century Ireland, selected a maidservant at evening prayers to accompany him to bed as his hot-water bottle, justifying the oddity on the scriptural precedent of King David. The 14th Baron Berners chose to irritate his neighbours by erecting at great expense a useless tower. A cat-lover held up the rebuilding of Coventry by refusing to vacate his house on the grounds that his two hundred flea-infested companions would suffer distress if they were moved.

As a housemaster is no doubt obliged to be, Frig Allt was milder in his eccentricities. Clean and fair-haired, with untidy shirt collars, he had a particular stride, moving swiftly and swinging a little from side to side. His biggish face was unobtrusively handsome, the kind of looks that fade in the memory because they don't register strongly at the time. He smoked a large pipe, sometimes cigarettes, and drank a great deal of water. His abstracted air was attributed to the fact that he was known to be working on the variorum edition of W.B. Yeats, having already assisted in the editing of the Collected Poems.

One of his colleagues held that the only way to keep the upper hand was, each year in each class, to pick on a boy who threatened to give trouble and blame him for everything whether he was guilty or not. Others let the upper hand slip from them; others again were born with authority and didn't have to think about such matters. Frig Allt, massively bored by classrooms and housemasterly duties, kept himself going through his oddities.

On a bitter January day he would enter a classroom and order the windows to be thrown open. Often he taught from outside one of these windows, wrapped in his voluminous gown, rasping out French *dictée* from a patch of grass. When I once admired a tie he was wearing he took it off and gave it to me. When I admired a small picture he possessed he gave it to me also. He had been known to sit on the ledge of the mantelpiece in the masters' common room to see if anyone would notice. At Trinity he had discovered an ancient privilege that permitted scholars to play marbles on the Dining Hall steps. He indulged himself at once.

On summer afternoons, in the company of a biographer of Yeats, whose younger son was at the school, Frig Allt would watch cricket. The biographer had an interest in the game, he none at all. But the occasion provided an opportunity for conversation about the poet, and Allt was expert at closing his mind to what he did not wish to enter it: the flannelled figures might not have existed.

On the point of being expelled for a misdemeanour too heinous for caning, a boy called Trench and I approached him in his housemaster's sitting-room, seeking his intervention on our behalf. He was lying on the floor at the foot of a bookcase, concerned — so he said — about the bookworms that were attacking his books.

'We wondered, sir, if you know what's going to happen to us,' Trench began, and Frig Allt replied that it was a serious business when microbes got going on your bookshelves.

'It's just that it would be a help to know,' Trench began again, but the only response he received was that people didn't believe bookworms existed. We went away.

That abstracted air, and his ploys to keep boredom at bay, made him what he was. At roll-call he adopted, for certain names, a nasal,

American drawl in order to ring the changes. He pointed out to a boy called Orr that the extra 'r' in his name was unnecessary, that the name would be more interesting without it. Without it, he added, the boy himself might in time become more interesting, and suggested that it was certainly worth experimenting in this direction. He watched a hole forming in the floorboards of his room when coals fell out of the fire, forgetting that when this happens you are meant to do something about it.

The tedium of communal life drove him away from the school, and into another, where he hoped his duties would be fewer. They weren't, and he managed only a few years there before he left schoolmastering altogether. Driven by his scholarship, he had a way, as he once said himself, of passing on.

He did so for the last time while still a young man, when his abstracted air got the better of him in London and he stepped out of the wrong side of a South Western electric train, his variorum unfinished. Hearing about the incident, it was easy to imagine, and still is: his pipe alight, he hums a tune as he prepares his stride for a platform that is not there.

His death accentuated what was not always self-evident: that there was nothing ersatz about his eccentricity. He died as he lived: somewhere else at the time.

(1991)

Long Stewart

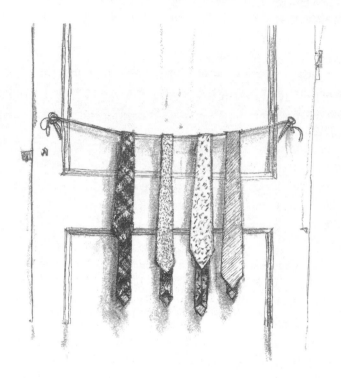

A TALL BOY places a selection of ties on a string looped between two drawing-pins on the inside of a wardrobe door. The ties are of finely woven tweed, green flecked with blue, orange and brown and purple. They have been purchased that afternoon on the way through Dublin and will not be worn until the term ends. Today is the term's first day, 12 January 1943.

The wardrobes in the upper dormitory are narrow plywood lockers, back to back, ranged down the middle of the room. The beds are foot to foot, running the length of the dormitory also. Each bed has a blue woollen cover, the repetition creating a uniformity that is emphasised throughout the school — in grey flannel shirts, in gowns and surplices and sober Sunday suits, in the yellow hue of the Tuesday pudding, in the peremptory tone of rules and regulations. Glen is the hearty house, Grange the arty one. Stackallan is the compromise house, its house-tie compromise grey.

'Ah,' the tall boy greets me in the Stackallan dormitory. I am new, knowing nothing yet of anything.

We exchange names. In an adult way he stretches out a hand. Boys do not do that; it is most unusual.

He is Stewart, K.J. Kenneth Stewart. Stewart major. Long Stewart, the playful geography master has named him, not to be confused with Villiers Stuart or Goldfish Stewart, or Dull Stewart from somewhere in Antrim. His wavy fair hair is parted in the middle; his square features, unblemished by spots or acne, give the impression of having always been shaved. He is immaculately turned out. Too tall to look anything but ridiculous in the statutory school cap, he has obtained permission not to wear it: his bedside locker contains a brown felt hat. At sixteen, nothing about him is boyish. He is a masher, putting on the style.

Victoria Four-Thirty is the novel he talks about, by Cecil Roberts, marvellous. Francis Brett Young is recommended also, and Walpole and Cronin and *Jamaica Inn*. Later there is the discovery of *Cakes and Ale* and *The Moon and Sixpence*, then *Crome Yellow* and *Brideshead Revisited*. He has learned by heart the end of *The Bridge of San Luis Rey*. 'We ourselves shall be loved for a while and forgotten. But the love will have been enough . . . There is a land of the living and a land of the dead, and the bridge is love, the only survival, the only meaning.' As a classroom subject, only English interests him. He would like to write himself. He begins to read Rupert Brooke.

As I am, he is a small-town provincial, but the home life he talks about is vastly different from my own. He takes out girls — bank clerks five or six years older than he is, who've even been engaged, girls from Sligo and Carrick-on-Shannon, girls on holiday at Rosses Point. His own town is Boyle in County Roscommon, famous for its excessive number of pubs. There are dances and a tennis club. He is good at tennis, and can dance.

We walk on Sunday afternoons down the long front drive, along the road to the Tibradden post-box, returning by the back drive because it makes a change. He is not one for tramping the hills or climbing to the top of Kilmasogue, nor for fried food in Farmer's, nor a bottle of stout in Lamb Doyle's. He is cautious about breaking rules: bending over to be caned by a smirking prefect seems as ridiculous as having to wear the school cap. He manages in the rough and tumble that reigns, conceding without regret that the time and place belong, not to him, but to the clever and the sporty and the ambitious. He is, he insists, only good at tennis.

He's funny, not as a stand-up comic is, nor with the perpetual sharpness of a wit, but as a purveyor of the quirky remark, the outraged point of view. Comment trickles from him, foibles fascinate his curiosity. He pretends a properness. He adopts a solemn stance. These are the governors of his humour, the straight face of its manic content. But laughter explodes often from beneath that surface and becomes infectious: such humour energises him, raising him from the lassitude that exasperates his mentors.

'A most dissipated person,' he answers my new boy's query about some passing figure. 'Dissolute' describes another; 'appalling' is reserved for loutish adolescence at its most graceless. His dissection of the school establishes a perspective: considered against the backdrop of Boyle society, it can't be taken too seriously, neither its *mores* nor its sillinesses; best just to make the days pass as agreeably as the days themselves allow. When he is teased it's hesitantly done: under that languid exterior, there's a warning that you tread carefully with a sophisticate.

But sometimes his grown-upness and his properness collapse. He fools about; he holds the floor in the brief interval between classes: suddenly on his feet, he plays an imaginary trombone or saxophone in the style of a swing musician. Lips tightly engaged on the mouthpiece, hands darting swiftly in the air, he is Artie Shaw and then Glen Miller, a suede shoe tapping while a moaning rhythm emerges perfectly in tune. 'Lay dat pistol down, babe,' he croons. 'Pistol-packin' momma, lay dat pistol down.' His suave figure sways and gyrates until it's brought to a halt by an unamused instruction citing page and line of Caesar's Gallic Wars.

He does not, himself, see much point in the information to be gleaned from this ancient aggression, any more than he sees the point of establishing that, if multiplied by itself, a given side of a triangle equals the sum of its two other sides when similarly multiplied. *And then there was a ghastly smell*, he sums up the outcome of a chemical experiment.

He avoids the intellectually arrogant, the affected, the gangs. Confident in his gregariousness, he addresses the more approachable of the

masters on equal terms, asking about girls, enquiring after wives. He sees
no reason why he should contribute to the St Patrick's Day tradition of
planting potatoes, since this is meant to be voluntary. He doesn't mind
standing out a bit, though not too much. There's timidity there too.

Films are what we talk about as much as novels. *The Grapes of Wrath,
For Whom the Bell Tolls, State Fair.* Tennis stars feature in his side of the
conversation also — Yvon Petra, Pauline Betz, Geoff Brown — and it's
for his services as a tennis-player that he is permitted, at last, to abandon
the grey Stackallan house-tie for the breezier green-and-white stripes of
the colours one. But tennis — being off-form at the net, foot-faulting,
poor returns — also feeds his gloom. Black moods are blacker in
summer, touchiness more often dominant. Stung by one of the playful
geography master's taunts, he maintains a dignified, cold response for
days or even weeks, choosing not to be on speaking terms with the
man except to meet the official requirements of the classroom. Should
the object of displeasure be a friend rather than a master, all joking and
laughter cease and the relationship is strained.

These schooldays end. 'Thank God for that,' Long Stewart remarks
urbanely at the last breakfast. His pressed flannels are noticeable among
the food-stained jackets and trousers ripped at the pockets, the trailing
shoe-laces and frayed cuffs. He comments for the last time on our
schooldays, then goes without sentiment. Others will return, to see
how the old place is getting on without them. He does not intend to,
and never does.

★

The family business in Boyle, once productive and well-to-do, is less
so now. One part of it — a corn mill — is prosperous still. But the
other side of things — the supply of electricity to the town — is shaky.
It is the last private plant in Ireland, an anachronism that has survived
the Shannon Scheme, the system inaugurated in the nineteen thirties to
become the country's national grid. *We're doing our best to keep the lights
on,* his letters say, the statement acquiring a doleful echo over the years.

The lights in fact go out: the plant is taken over and all that's left
is an electrical goods shop. He sends a cutting of a film review he has
written for the local paper and adds that he has become an agent for
Exide batteries, and 'employed by the Royal Irish Automobile Club to
inspect hotels. Unpaid except for perks.'

In the café of the Adelphi Cinema in Dublin we sit with the fiancée he has driven over from County Roscommon so that I may meet her: Ingrid, a German au pair girl, employed in the household of a local commercial traveller. She is understandably bewildered by Irish small-town priorities, and by the lifestyle of her employers, Mr and Mrs McIlhoney, and the many McIlhoney children. We draw her attention to the cinema manager, in evening dress at four o'clock in the afternoon, and bewilder her further by revealing that this man was once a master at school. We tell her about Des Malley, who was a master also until he was sacked, who used to say that being in love was like having hot raspberry jam poured down the back of your neck. We recall the Sunday evening in Chapel when an odour of regurgitated brandy suddenly enriched the air, to the sound of heaving evacuation.

'Oh, my God!' Long Stewart murmurs, and for no single reason we begin to laugh as we used to on the road to the Tibradden post-box, with abandon we can't control. And the girl he is to marry laughs too, in that same way.

*

Later letters say the tennis club isn't what it used to be. They tell of friends departing the town, cousins settling in England, of change and marriages, his own to Ingrid among them. He inherits the electricity shop. He is a businessman, dependable and conscientious. But the shop is small, and competition is no respecter of human attributes beyond those that have to do with convenience. The Exide franchise is a help.

In childhood and youth the little town of Boyle has been the backdrop to his life. Now, in middle age, he is unique there, his dress sense and his courtesy standing out, as they did at school. He is well liked, known to everyone and knowing everyone in turn. President of the Chamber of Commerce, he keeps in check his brooding introspection. His neat pipe, his gin and tonic, his laughter, belie a self-tormenting nature that hasn't changed.

Yet the contradiction is that he's a happy man, as happy in his melancholy as in anything that delights him. He deplores provincial life while managing well enough in it. Deploring is still part of him; it still makes a wag of him. You laugh with him or at him: old friends are permitted to have that either way.

And then one Sunday evening — 29 May 1989 — he is no longer there. *A quiet and unassuming man of gentlemanly behaviour,* the local paper says. His fellow shopkeepers close their doors as the funeral passes. Wreaths come in from everywhere.

(1991)

Alma Mater

I MET MY tutor once. He was a precise man, with shiny black hair carefully brushed, a reader in law, later no doubt a professor.

'So you've changed your mind?' he commented in economical tones, his dark legal eyes displaying for an instant a hint of the sigh he successfully suppressed.

'Well, yes,' I agreed. I was attempting to extricate myself from the Medical School, in which I had erroneously landed myself.

'Actually there's no difficulty about that.' There was a cautious nod, the motion suggesting that the statement was made without prejudice, that no precedent had been established. 'The question is, what now?'

'That's what I wanted to ask you, sir.'

'You mean, you don't know what you want to do?'

'Well no, sir, actually.'

'You could try Modern Languages. Presumably you are acquainted with the rudiments of French, for instance? Or Irish?'

'It's not possible to do English on its own?'

'No, it isn't.' There was a pause. Other suggestions were put forward. Then: 'A lot of the undecided go in for the Church.'

'I don't think I'm cut out —'

'Come back when you've made up your mind.'

I never did. 'What are you doing?' people would ask me during that first term and I would say nothing, which was approximately correct because the few lectures I attended — in preparation for Littlego, an examination in general subjects, obligatory for all students — were not exacting. When, occasionally, I noticed the neat presence of my tutor in the distance I hurried out of sight.

Trinity College, Dublin, was founded in the reign of Elizabeth I, in 1592. It is the single college of Dublin University, its buildings and playing fields spread over forty-two acres in the centre of the capital. Such largesse of space, and the site occupied, lend Trinity a certain grandeur and, in this joint respect only, give it the edge over the colleges of Oxford and Cambridge. The year of my arrival was 1946, and although the fag-ends of privilege and the Ascendancy order were of little significance in day-to-day life they had not yet been completely swept aside. There was still a hint of the Big House in academe. The cobbled Front Square slowed down the bustle of contemporary time.

It does so still, and Burke and Goldsmith still loftily evoke the grace of another generation. But the changes of nearly half a century have since imbued those scraps of the past with an antiquated feel. Botany Bay — Trinity's largest residential area — was as grim in 1946 as its title suggests: a vast expanse of mud where today there are tennis-courts. The inspiration of Henry Moore is compensation now for an ugly campanile. Contemporary architecture challenges the old library and shows up the less compelling Graduates' Memorial Building.

The grey façades are white now, but the Rubrics are as cosy on the eye as ever. Less so, still, is W.E.H. Lecky on his plinth, and Geo. Salmon, Provost, 1888–1904. The high blue-faced clocks are as they always were, but the porters' caps, like jockeys' once, suggest the *gendarmerie* now. At the huge Front Gate, where the porters rule, Club news is pinned up in the same dusty glass cases, but where there should be tidings from the Dublin University mission fields the details of an eating contest are announced. The Camogie Club is new.

In other ways, too, continuity has been broken. In 1946 Trinity was firmly Protestant. Catholics who wished to study there had to obtain dispensation from their bishops, and this wasn't always forth-coming. But fees had to be gathered from somewhere, and in that edgy post-war period they came from British ex-servicemen who found their own universities full. They were joined by Americans, Poles, Egyptians, Nigerians, Belgians, Canadians, Indians, Australians, and many others. Trinity thrived.

But we local Irish, while not outnumbered, were dwarfed by the sophistication and worldliness of men returned from battle. They sported moustaches, often wives, and even babies. They played bridge, gave cocktail parties, trotted girls off to the basement café of Switzer's, to the International bar, or the Dog and Waffle for lunch. The English ones said 'actually' with a drawl that delighted Dublin's street urchins. Understandably they made us feel like the schoolboys we had so recently been.

★

I was at Trinity unwillingly and hoped to pass through it unnoticed. I found digs in a lodging-house in Blackrock where Scotch terriers were bred. Its rooms had a ragged appearance, caused by the shredding of chair-covers and curtains by these animals; a doggy odour, pervasive everywhere, occasionally emanated from the food. Elderly women were my fellow-boarders and some time in the past one of them — the late Mrs Mosse — had been quite badly gnawed, an incident that was regularly touched upon by her survivors.

At the end of my first term I couldn't afford to keep my room on during the Christmas vacation, and when I returned to Dublin in

January had to find another. The long snow of 1947 — which didn't properly thaw until St Patrick's Day — had already begun. I trudged the streets because I couldn't afford buses and eventually found a room in Terenure, with a family called Finnegan. It was cheaper than the Blackrock one because I cooked for myself. Cooking, though, wasn't easy: Mr Finnegan was a 'glimmer man' — an inspector employed by Dublin Gas to detect the illegal tapping of any residue of gas in the pipes during the hours when it was forbidden to use it in those austere post-war years. He was a stern, pernickety man, who kept a watchful eye, not just on the gas pipes but on life itself, which he liked to order on his own terms. His wife, a naturally modest woman in whom he had instilled a further degree of humility, went in dread of him.

In the middle of one night I accidentally set the chimney of my room on fire and as I listened to it roaring I recalled how Kitty, our maid, used to throw paraffin up a chimney and light it to burn off the soot. Cheaper than a chimney sweep, Kitty used to say. I imagined the blaze would stop, as Kitty's always did, but in fact it didn't. Mrs Finnegan arrived in her nightclothes, terrified in case her husband woke up. She fetched a stirrup pump and together we squirted it up the chimney, covering the floor of my room with dirty water on which the remnants of the papers I'd been burning now floated. When the blaze was extinguished mops and buckets were fetched, Mrs Finnegan creeping up and down the dark staircase, fearful of lighting it in case, waking for a moment, her husband noticed the gleam beneath his door. For hours we spoke in whispers and tiptoed about. Then I made tea and we had it at the table. I emptied out a bag of broken biscuits, which we dunked in our tea to soften the sound of eating them. She would have to wear mittens at breakfast, Mrs Finnegan whispered, to hide the grime she couldn't get off her hands. We drank more tea and ate more biscuits, and neither of us said what was uppermost in our minds: that there was something exciting about sitting there at five-fifteen in the morning, deceiving a sleeping tyrant.

Soon after that everything changed. I was allocated rooms in College and, *faute de mieux*, I enrolled in the History School. Anonymity was impossible now. Evening Commons had to be attended. The Junior Dean's permission had to be obtained if I wished to entertain a member of the opposite sex, as girls were called. A limitation was placed on the number of evenings each week I might be outside the gates after nine o'clock. There was the ceremony of the once-a-week bath in the communal bath-house. Chapel was obligatory.

But the saving grace of institutional life is the variety of people who constitute it, and in this respect Trinity was not lacking. There was the ageing student who had been there for longer than any of the porters could remember, and the one who broke into the printing press in order to peruse the examination papers, and the one who went in for blackmail, causing a hitherto respectable medical doctor to emigrate to the antipodes. The Pope O'Mahony was perpetually in search of a bed, a girl kept a cat on a lead, another was called Marmalade because of her hair. A lively Divinity student snipped the hair of the man in front of him during *Scott of the Antarctic*. We old Columbans stuck together and were no doubt considered snobbish.

Authority was intimidating, as of right. Lost in their higher thoughts, all weariness and dignity, stern stately figures daily traversed the Front Square cobbles. The Boadicea of the History School went fearsomely by, protected by the wide brim of her hat from the presumption of greeting or recognition. An ancient cleric prided himself on an ability to make girls cry during *viva voce* encounters. Vengeance was exacted in a grisly manner: one of them was murdered.

On the other hand, there was the nice old boy you hoped you'd get when it came to displaying your familiarity with Horace or Pliny. 'I'm afraid we didn't do that bit, sir,' you would apologetically regret when he indicated a passage you could not recall from Dr Giles's Keys to the Classics. And then, lowering the voice: 'There were girls in the class, sir.'

A small, excitable man who lectured in a staccato manner often arrived in the lecture-hall in a state of mild undress, occasionally unshaven. This was R.B. McDowell, amusing and erudite at the same time, who would talk to anyone, and when lacking a companion, to himself. Wrapped in a heavy black overcoat, he wandered about the college buildings at night, muttering in a fevered manner about the viceroyalty of Lord Townshend or Gladstone's second Land Act. 'A penny for the waiter,' he would calculate the tip if he took you for coffee in Jury's Hotel, then on the other side of College Green. The story was later told of how on his first visit to London, which he believed to be a particularly immoral city, he hurried through the streets protesting 'No, thank you, madam,' to any woman who even vaguely crossed his path.

He talked compulsively, had a prodigious memory, and later became a television personality.

His colleague, Dr Moody, head of the History department, gave parties. In his house in Rathgar we stood about listening to the Pastoral Symphony, after which there was a spread of sandwiches and cake in the dining-room, with tea or 'cup'. Dr Moody didn't seem much at home during these occasions, except when engaged in scholarly exchanges with First Class material. Queuing on the small landing outside the lavatory, the rest of us would do our best to conduct a more down-to-earth conversation as he hovered politely. I noticed tomatoes growing in his garden and remarked how well they appeared to be ripening. I asked him if he fertilised them with blood, which was a fashion then, but he replied that carrying buckets of blood from a butcher's shop was not something he would relish, so that was the end of that. Downstairs, his wife remarked to the girls that if any of them ever felt like looking in on a Saturday night they might care to listen to Saturday Night Theatre with her, and afterwards discuss it. This was my first experience of a certain kind of academic household, and the birth of a claustrophobia that invariably returns in such surroundings. Yet Dr Moody and his wife meant well, and harmed no one.

*

In my rooms in Botany Bay I carved the 1939–45 war memorial for St Anne's in Dawson Street, and cut the letters on a gravestone. My brother, who worked in an architect's office, shared these rooms until the authorities questioned his presence. Apart from Irish History, which reads like a good novel, I was unable to develop an interest in the discipline I had chosen, but there were many compensations: Maurice O'Brien at the Gate, F.J. McCormick at the Abbey, the Municipal Art Gallery, Jack Yeats at Waddington's, dancing girls at the Capitol and the Royal. From that good address in the heart of Dublin I came to know the city by wandering through it in the small hours of the morning. In the Coombe and the Liberties the dark was cheered by conversations with a perambulating garda; on the quays with the last of the night ladies — the best remembered a one-legged dressmaker from Cabra.

Public-house evenings ended in the Crystal Ballroom or out in Goatstown on the bona fide, and images of barmen are vivid to this day. Gaunt, bespectacled, with a popping Adam's apple, the one in the upstairs lounge of Mooney's in College Street eerily resembled de Valera, and added a surreal quality to the illusion by repeating, as a sort of *leit-motif*, the selling message of a radio advertisement. 'Bird's Custard and Bird's Jelly de luxe,' he would endlessly intone in high-pitched mimicry. 'You do want the best, don't you?'

Mr Dowd in Baggot Street, aproned and enormous, kept a sedate house. 'Three stout by the neck,' a stranger to his ways might order, but Mr Dowd did not permit opened bottles to be handed across his bar. When glasses were replenished it must be in an orderly fashion, the bottles poured by himself or his staff. 'Tip for the barman at all?' the boy in Ryan's would hopefully suggest at the end of an evening, but the

hint was never taken. Tom McAuley in Rathmines kept a greyhound in the Gents.

Some time in October 1950 I hired the required evening attire from an outfitter in Hawkins Street and received a degree. I sold my gown to the porter I had bought it from four years before and walked away, aware that I had made little of, and contributed nothing to, university life. When I go back now to stroll about the old buildings and the new ones, it is always with a sense of regret.

(1992)

Visitors in Dublin

'Ah, but she was the queer old skeowsha anyhow, Anna Livia, trinket-toes! And sure he was the quare old buntz too, Dear Dirty Dumpling, foostherfather of fingalls and dotthergills. Gammer and gaffer we're all their gangsters.'

JAMES JOYCE.

THE FIRST TIME I was a visitor in Dublin it was noisy and hot and crowded. I had been told to wait outside Barrett's in Grafton Street in my unpleasant flannel hat that was considered stylish for the city. The trams went clattering by, and when I became impatient with the frustration of just standing there I threw the flannel hat under one of them. I was five or so at the time. Earlier that day my father had driven the wrong way down that same street. 'Well, sure, you got there,' the Guard on point duty at the bottom said, 'and isn't that the main thing?'

Although he was unfamiliar with the city's traffic regulations, my father knew the waiters and the porters in the Wicklow Hotel by name, and from exchanges with an acquaintance in the hall or the bar marvellous-sounding titles floated down to me: Ballylooby Boy, Rackety Lassie, Salt of the Earth, all of which were noted on the back of a Sweet Afton packet. In Robt. Roberts' Café there were huge coffee- and tea-urns on the counter, and a trio of ladies played waltzes and foxtrots. Jimmy O'Dea, the funniest man in Ireland, was at the Gaiety Theatre, just round the corner.

The Mills of God Grind Slowly But They Grind Exceeding Small, a high reminder insisted, not far from the Bleeding Horse public house. And a real horse slithered beneath its load and had to be rescued from the shafts, noisily teased on to its feet again by men who'd been playing pitch and toss. My father brought me into Davy Byrne's, telling me it was a famous bar.

I did not know then that the black pool of Dublin was a Viking foundation, later to become the centre of the sophisticated English Pale. 'The seat of this city is on all sides pleasant, comfortable, and wholesome,' remarked an earlier visitor to the city. 'If you would traverse the hills, they are not far off . . . If you will take a view of the sea, it is at hand.' Add to this the Georgian splendour of squares and thoroughfares and there is Dublin in its later heyday — the 'grey brick upon brick' that Louis MacNeice wrote of, destined to become 'the bare bones of a fanlight / Over a hungry door'.

Not all visitors to Dublin have agreed with the view of the sixteenth-century enthusiast. Dr Johnson was grudging: 'Dublin, though a place much worse than London, is not as bad as Iceland.' A nameless traveller noted that: 'Many of its inhabitants call this city Divlin, quasi Divels Inn, and very properly it is by them so termed; for there is hardly a city in the world that entertains such variety of devil's imps as that doth. If any knavishly break, murder, rob, or are desirous of polygamy, they straightway repair thither, making that place . . . their asylum, or sanctuary.'

Dean Swift might not have disagreed. Certainly, in his more melancholy moments, he revealed dissatisfaction: he was obscure in the solitude of his cathedral close; no one wished to hear about his state of health; his life was no one's concern; his hearse would inspire no tears; and while he lived, there were the city's awful irritations, street cries in particular.

> And therefore till our law-makers shall think it proper to interpose so far as to make these traders pronounce their words in such terms that a plain Christian hearer may comprehend what is cried, I would advise all newcomers to look out at their garret windows, and there see whether the thing that is cried be tripes or flummery, buttermilk or cowheels . . . The affirmation solemnly made in the cry of herrings is directly against all truth and probability: 'Herrings alive, alive here.' The very proverb will convince us of this; for what is more frequent in ordinary speech than to say of some neighbour for whom the passing bell rings that he is 'dead as a herring'.

In more senses than one Swift's Dublin is as dead as the herrings

he complains about. For in spite of the architectural riches that still evoke its imperial past, Dublin today is the Dublin left behind after Ireland's terrible beauty was born; since 1916, what occurred then on its streets has mattered more than the gracious backdrop of Trinity or the Bank of Ireland, Merrion or Fitzwilliam. It is a forgotten footnote now that riots greeted the Custom House and the Four Courts when first they etched the city's skyline. Instead, what has passed into popular mythology are memories of the blasting of the General Post Office and events at Boland's Mills, of death and surrender among the debris of revolution. Long before, Thomas Carlyle predicted that Dublin would be one of the breaking points of feudalism in Western Europe: he was now proved right. An era ended with a vengeance and a bang when Dubliners finally took to the streets, but the spirit that inspired them had been smouldering long before the first shot was fired.

'During the eighteenth century,' Stephen Gwynn has written,

> Dublin was one of the most notable capitals of Europe. It was inhabited by a rich aristocracy, who spent money lavishly on themselves and showed also a fine taste in the provision of public buildings. But

their relation to the Irish people at large was even more distant than that of the Russian aristocrats before the revolution; they were divided from them by religion as well as by class, and there could therefore be no national expression . . . After the Union in 1800 the legislature was withdrawn and the wealthy element transferred itself to London. Dublin became during the nineteenth century the centre of a continuous revolutionary movement to recover its position as, in the full sense, an Irish capital.

In the square, grey Abbey Theatre Sean O'Casey re-told the story of the rising in human terms. Urban and vernacular, his voice seemed vastly different from those who had already retailed the peasant tales, or legendary heroics, of the Celtic Twilight. In fact, O'Casey was presenting the other side of the same coin: another aftermath of suppression and frustration. In Dublin the tricolour waved now; the Soldier's Song had come to stay; the damaged city was rebuilt. The names of some streets, chosen at random almost, were changed; some statues of imperial figures were carted off, others left; the red pillar-boxes were painted green, while retaining the royal insignia. The travel writer H.A. Piehler noticed, as a sign of the new régime, 'the prevalence of betting offices and the universal procurability of sweepstake tickets'. But even without the face-lift, and the bundling away of stuffy rules and regulations, Dublin was coming into its own anyway. Eblana to the Romans, later the Town of the Ford of Hurdles — as it is in Irish today — it was finally beginning to feel at one with itself.

V.S. Pritchett, visiting Dublin for the first time during the 1920s, fell under the spell that freedom induced, even while the Civil War lumbered on. It

got a decisive hold of me in the next two days as I walked about the comfortable little Georgian and early Victorian city, where the red brick and the brown were fresher and less circumspect than the brick of London. The place seemed to be inhabited only by lawyers and doctors. The mists of the bog on which it is built softened the air. Complexions were delicate, eyes were alive with questions. As you passed people in the street they seemed to pause with expectation, hoping for company, and with the passing gaiety of hail and farewell, with the emphasis particularly on the latter. There was a longing for

75

passing acquaintance; and an even stronger longing for your back to be turned, to give a bit of malice a chance.

Twenty years later, alone and brooding in Winetavern Street, a visitor liked the city no better than the one who found it full of devil's imps, designating it the most miserable town he had ever spent a night in. That there was a renowned pub life, and singing till the small hours, impressed him hardly at all. Nor did convenient horse-racing on a Saturday afternoon, nor greyhound racing, nor the attempted martyrdom of Cosmas and Damian as interpreted by Fra Angelico. The dead were marvellously preserved in a quayside vault. There was the great Book of Kells, the Ardagh Chalice, the three-card trick so skilfully performed at a street corner it was a pleasure to watch. In the Fun Palace on Burgh Quay you could roll pennies and win a prize if one landed favourably; you could operate a miniature crane that dipped into an assortment of celluloid toys and confectionery; and the fruit machines weren't called one-arm bandits yet. There were Palm Grove ice-cream parlours, and the Inkspots at the Four Provinces dancehall. It might even still be true, as it was in Bishop Berkeley's day, that more money circulated at Dublin's card-tables than at all the fairs of Ireland.

But for the solitary traveller none of that is a consolation, for an element in any city's life is the loneliness that awaits the stranger, and the more there is on offer the less any of it suits. Cities are always in a hurry; companionship isn't easy to come by. The visitor mooches round the Botanic Gardens, and is beady-eyed and critical in crowded places. Your first day in Dublin is always your worst, John Berryman noticed. Those wise Victorians, Mr and Mrs Hall, had each other for company.

I have myself remained a visitor in Dublin for a lifetime. Years of schooling there, of university, of being employed there and living there, have not altered that. It is said that once a city is a capital it is everybody's. Natives and visitors stake different claims and offer different perspectives: muddle makes cities what they are. This may be true, but in this present case it doesn't seem entirely so: Dublin belongs to Dubliners.

As a schoolboy, I met them for the first time — sharp-witted, sharp-tongued, sharp in appearance even. The provincial is no match for these wily locals; this is their place and still their Pale. 'Dublin jackeens,' you might say in County Cork or County Wexford: you kept the expression to yourself in O'Connell Street.

You have to walk to get to know a city: it was then — in the Dublin of the 1940s — that I first discovered that. Harcourt Street was a staid row of unlicensed hotels, politely elbowing one another for attention; Henry Street was famous for its sausage shop. The Mansion House set the tone in Dawson Street, and Charlemont Street offered a display of corns, extracted from the footsore: *The Walker's Friend*, a notice said. Marrowbone Lane and Lad Lane and Lady Lane, Ebenezer Terrace and Morning Star Road: all of them had an echo of a lost significance. In back-street sweetshops sunlight fell on Peggy's Leg and pink money-balls, and drained the colour from the wrappings of Rainbow Toffees, and caught the dust on the white sugar mice that were known as royal mice.

In one of Clery's windows a hypnotised man slept deeply on the mattress he advertised. In Great Longford Street the houses of the well-to-do were now the tenements of the poor. Rags filled the smashed panes of McNeice's fanlights. The air was pungent with the smell of poverty.

On Sundays, flags and favours made their way to Croke Park for another all-Ireland final. On weekdays people hurried on the Ha'penny Bridge, not bothering to linger over the view. I didn't know when I passed a house in Mary Street that this was where Michael Collins had his closest shave. Nor that Oliver St John Gogarty had presented the Liffey with his gift of swans at Islandbridge.

Cinemas were everywhere in the 1940s, in business as never before or since. The Metropole, the Grand Central, the Adelphi; the Carlton for Abbot and Costello, the Savoy for Norman Metcalf on the organ and the singsong words handwritten on the screen, the Corinthian for cowboys. *Escape to Happiness* was at the Grafton, *La Femme du Boulanger* ran for months at the Astor— a favourite rendezvous for lovers, some of the seats being miniature sofas. The ice-cream girl at the Green was on for anything.

The last tram rattled on the rails. Years later Nelson was toppled from his high pillar, smashed to smithereens; they took away the Bovril sign and the sky was different at night. Then developers arrived to tear at Dublin's heart, and petty crime to soil its style; congestion robbed it of its easy-going pace. Nightspots and discos came, and launderettes and Bar-B-Q takeaways, and brisk little cafés and serious restaurants. Joy-riders rampaged, drug peddlers tempted, walkie-talkies disturbed the peace. And the fashion in insurance-company architecture brought the melancholy nothingness that is the twentieth century's ugliest trade mark.

Yet in the midst of all this disturbance the heart of Dublin survives, nourished by its shades of Thomas Davis and poor Robert Emmet, Molly Malone and Biddy Mulligan, Wolfe Tone and patient Henry Grattan. Above the sluggish crawl of the river, in early-morning air that's acrid with the smell of brewing, seagulls still screech, still perch on the quayside parapets. The sun is bright on the ageing limestone of O'Connell Street while it warms the city's new dignitaries and the new Crazy Janes of its streets. Beggars share, as they always have, a lean hospitality with tipsters and musicians and pickpockets, traders and general loiterers, and a sprinkling of street-walkers, whom Dublin from time to time pretends do not exist. 'We make do with our own wives in this town,' was the severe reprimand once offered to an unfortunate Englishman — a traveller in cardboard — who sought the solace of the fleshpots.

Today, as in the recent or the distant past, this is a city notable for chance encounters. In Merrion Row or Nassau Street, or anywhere at all, a face in the crowd is suddenly familiar. Polite exchanges as to health, and the weather remarked upon, preface the repairing to Toner's or O'Neill's or wherever's at hand. And when you're back on the streets again the tinker children are waiting, waggling their damp cardboard boxes at you. Shawled women press in to offer prayers for your spiritual well-being. 'Excuse me, sir' — in hushed tones, men outside turf accountants' declare themselves temporarily embarrassed. The price of a cup of tea, the bus fare to Dalkey: a loan until Friday, repayment where we stand, same time, on the dot.

Survival is nourished all over again, day in day out, in the chatter that enlivens the velvet-clad cubicles of Bewley's cafés, in the timeless shout of the evening paperboys, in the mundane quality of Dublin's mood. Hard facts are what matter here, and the hard facts of Dublin are that no city has better barmen, that no city is as quick on the uptake or as swift with a loaded riposte. Pretension is forgiven only when accompanied by wit; self-admiration has a short life. It's as disputatious a place as ever it was, its gossip as merciless, its snobberies as peculiar to itself.

Given to the grand gesture, it welcomes back its sporting heroes in lavish style; and just for fun it changes, again, the colour of its buses. There's a swiftness to condemn, especially when condemnation seems like a talking point. Emotions are volatile, yet opinions are rarely less than measured.

The raw excesses of commerce, the tattiness of money-grubbing, mock the elegance of old stone and brick. But architectural charm, for ever brushed down, can equally lead a city to the grave: Dublin's terraces and avenues, its courts and squares, at least do not sleep the sleep of a museum. Instead, they are threatened, squabbled over, assaulted, protected; and among them another generation become Dubliners.

The schoolgirls of Inchicore and Phibsborough, boys making their way in Quinnsworth, computer operators, the counter clerks of building societies and betting shops, are an army of bicycles on the weekday streets. They throng the Sunday nightclubs, with fashion-buyers and insurance salesmen, lorrymen and porters, nurses and shop assistants. They save for holidays in Santa Ponsa because there isn't enough sun in Bray or Salthill; because they like a touch of foreignness, but not

79

too much. They like a Margherita cocktail or a Fuzzy Navel, a Spanish pizza, the vino, an adventure. They know what they want, and see to it that they get it: their predecessors dreamed.

Briefly in St Stephen's Green a ghetto-blaster howls 'I Haven't the Time to Feel the Pain,' until a park attendant says no. Condoms are on sale. The pro-Life lobby is on the march, stolid-faced youths to the fore. A woman shakes her head at them, declaring they don't know what they're talking about, one of fourteen herself, too much for any woman to bear. A sorrowful man strides up and down outside the railings of Leinster House, his placard baldly stating: 'Career Ruined by Government Abuses.' A child robs in Talbot Street.

Change and the absence of it keep company in these broad and narrow streets where the girls are still pretty. 'They say the Chinaman eats the bamboo,' an elderly drinker remarked in a snug back bar forty years ago, apropos of nothing. 'Is that so?' is possibly still the response after due deliberation. Faces reflect faces that are there no more; voices echo voices. A pint of plain is still your only man. Dublin is its people.

(1988)

Summer, 1952

IT IS A world of gossip and small vendettas, of starched white undermatrons' uniforms, Kennedy's Latin primer. Dormitories honour Ralegh and Clive, Drake and Wellington, Nelson and Marlborough. *Paul est le fils de Monsieur et Madame Lépine.* Take two isosceles triangles. *Amo, amas, amat.*

Apply direct to the Headmaster, Gabbitas-Thring advise while reminding that ten per cent of the first term's salary is the agreed commission. If there's an interview, travelling expenses tend to be overlooked, but Gabbitas-Thring don't mention that.

Kipper Feet — also known as Ten-to-Two — doesn't address new masters for a year. 'I'll take showers,' Old Pastry offers, hurrying eagerly from a muddy rugby pitch. Five minutes later he enters Paradise, steam rising in the open shower-room, young bodies soaped. The staff-room's practical joker is good with disguised voices on the telephone, and releases hens in Old Pastry's bedroom while Old Pastry sleeps. There are new-boy ordeals and private games. On O.B. Day *The Mikado* is performed, in carpentry lessons bird-boxes are made.

The Classics master scribbles on sheets of foolscap in a bus shelter. Is he writing a book? Or surreptitious letters to one of the lady cooks, he being a married man? In the Dun Cow every evening his bachelor colleagues go over the ground carefully. Why write on foolscap in a bus shelter when there's a comfortable staff-room? After the Easter holidays one of the lady cooks does not return.

'We're going home,' is the theme song of *Staff Laughs* at the end of the autumn term. 'We're on the way that leads to home . . .' Miss Morrish, loyal school secretary for twenty-five years, keen on dramatics, unearths suitable farces for this Christmas treat. Miss Morrish has won accolades for her selected twenty minutes of *Rope* in a local one-act festival; she likes things properly done. 'We've seen the good things and the bad,' the staff-room lustily sing, Old Pastry at the piano. 'And now we're absolutely mad . . . We're g-o-i-n-g home . . .' Last year it was *Sussex by the Sea*.

At the Staff Dance, Brookie and Blondie, martinets of the lower forms, seethe with resentment because they're obliged to be present. Of a certain age, unsmiling faces beneath fluffy grey hair, they mutter into their cups of tea. Stout Mrs Spriggs, in charge of the masters' quarters — the Masteries they're known as — is resplendent in turquoise glitter and has had a glass or two of sherry. The headmaster's Second-in-Command dutifully takes the floor with one after another of the dining-room maids, who don't know what to say to him any more than he does to them. Kipper Feet lights up another pipeful of Three Nuns and praises the Conservative Party.

A recent old boy returns to join the staff. Too long in the Dun Cow, he pees into the staff-room fire, standing to win a shilling if he can put it out. The French master dislikes the history master, the history master dislikes the bursar, the bursar dislikes the P.T. instructor. Bungy Bodger, who's not much liked by anyone, draws attention to his spiked shoes, which once accompanied Bannister around an Oxford track. Kipper Feet's house is burgled, the missing ornament greeting him on the staff-room table when he arrives the next morning. 'We're on to you,' the disguised voice on the telephone warns, causing Old Pastry to replace the receiver hastily. Blue-blazered and serious, in scoutmaster's garb on Fridays, the Second-in-Command turns as blind an eye as he can manage to these staff-room pranks and feuds. His study is enlivened with woggles and camping-pegs, Baden-Powell above the mantelpiece. One day he would like to step into the headmaster's shoes, but everyone knows he never will.

In different schools one art room or another is my particular province — an outhouse, part of the stables, a one-time greenhouse — but my attempts to lie low in my unimportant area of the curriculum are not successful. A headmaster walks me up and down a narrow cinder path, cross because my request for a picture of the ugliest woman in the world has inspired the repeated likeness of his wife. In several instances a cigarette butt dangles surrealistically from one of her nostrils, which does not help matters. A hockey practice I'm in charge of is a shambles on one of those weekends when parents come.

Twenty years on, the greenhouse is still blisteringly hot in summer, the stables' outhouse freezing in winter. Haxby's crude chatter echoes, little Ryder's homesick tears drip all over his moated castle, Wooding spills the Indian ink on purpose. The girls from the sister school come — pretty Sarah, haughty Jane, angelic Frances, bossy Margaret, flirty Caroline. Podgy Diana paints herself dancing in front of the Queen. Susan has a tantrum because the colours of her hunting scene have run. Petrified at twelve and a half, their faces are effortlessly recalled.

But nothing of that time has lodged as firmly in the memory as the summer of 1952, when I was first introduced to that small, peculiar world, when Elm Park was gasping its last in County Armagh and I considered myself fortunate to be there.

★

The stationmaster at Killylea spoke of porridge in the plural. 'I'd rather have salt on them than sugar,' he used to say.

As small as a railway station can be, the railway station was a mile and a half from the village. Trains were not frequent, a couple a day. The stationmaster was on his own there, which may have accounted for his becoming out of touch with established speech. 'You can't beat the green Chivers' jelly,' he would say if you were waiting for a train, 'with a good dollop of cream on them.' One way or another the stationmaster told you a lot about the food he ate.

When you set off from the railway station to the village you noticed after about five minutes the gates of an avenue on your right. If you passed through them instead of continuing to Killylea you found yourself eventually at Elm Park. It was a gaunt, grey, good-looking Georgian house with a semi-circular sweep in front of it, and cropped lawns and shrubberies. It had belonged to one of those Anglo-Irish families that were rarer in Ulster during the Ascendancy's heyday than they were in the rest of Ireland.

Such houses have been down on their luck for most of this century, and Elm Park was no exception. As a preparatory school, its great conservatory was a place where afternoon drinks were given out — Quosh and Mi-Wadi and Kia-Ora — depending on the brand each of its twenty-two boys had handed in at the beginning of term. Its spacious bedrooms were dormitories, its double bathrooms useful on communal bath nights, the dining-room perfect for end-of-term theatricals. The ubiquitous white paint of wainscoting and doors was chipped and bruised, ceilings were dappled brown from dried-out damp. Rickety, well-inked desks and a varnished cupboard furnished the drawing-room. No claret aged softly in the cellars; Dinky cars made a dirt track round a summer-house.

Later, when I no longer knew Elm Park, its purpose changed again. Bankruptcy brought the school to an end in the mid-nineteen fifties, just as shrewd anticipation of the shape of things to come had brought the previous era to a close. The house was given over to chickens then, deep-litter birds roosting in the great conservatory and pecking each other in the drawing-room. So I was told, and the story has a ring of truth. Such houses, in Ireland and elsewhere, often end as tourist hotels, but since terrorism has had its way in Northern Ireland its attractions as a tourist playground have naturally been curtailed.

In the summer of 1952 I had no wish to go and live in a remote country house with twenty-two small boys, and colleagues who were an unknown quantity. I had, however, little option, having had my services rejected by sundry small businesses in Dublin — by auctioneers' salesrooms, estate agents, Thomas Cook, the Sun Life of Canada, the *Irish Times*, and a firm that manufactured telephone-booths. Briefly I had received a modest weekly wage in return for calling for a designated brand of beer in selected Northside public houses, whether as an encouragement to others or in an effort to establish if the beer was being stocked I never fully ascertained; and since inebriation invariably prevented me from accurately completing the forms I was provided with by the brewery, my assistance was soon dispensed with.

For a similarly brief period I'd had a job which I'd found in the situations vacant column of the *Irish Independent*. *Suit a Nun*, the advertisement ran. *Elderly or active*. After an initial hesitation I was accepted as second-best. For three pounds a week, inclusive of bus fares, I travelled daily from Dublin to a house in County Kildare in order to tutor a backward, left-handed child and her friend from next door. Within a couple of weeks the friend's younger brother joined this small academy, and for a time it seemed as if I had discovered the secret of making a living without undue exertion.

But in the end — like the failed Christian brother years ago in Tipperary — I couldn't manage on the money, which is how one of the two headmasters of Elm Park came to be interviewing me in a room he had somehow acquired access to, above the Front Square lavatories in Trinity College. He was a youngish man, no more than thirty-two or -three, with a long handsome face characterised by a suggestion of mild pomposity, hair parted in the middle. He was the Junior Partner, he explained, an emphasis in his tone supplying the capital letters. I didn't know at the time that he was as desperate for teaching assistance as I was for gainful employment.

'We have a Maths Man of course,' he said when we'd agreed that I should fill the vacancy, 'and we have our Bottom Form Mistress. At the other end of things the Old Man still pulls his weight.'

The more he spoke the more capital letters there were. No doubt perfected in conversations with prospective parents, the Junior Partner's mode of speech made Elm Park — school, house and setting — sound exquisitely grand, each reference leaving behind it an impression of splendour and luxury. A gloss of considerable importance was attached to the staff positions he spoke of, and although this managed to survive the consideration that he had just engaged me to fill one of them, it looked distinctly questionable when he revealed that due to unforeseen circumstances there was, as yet, no second assistant master for the term that began in two days' time. There was, when it came to the point, no Maths Man.

'Devil to get hold of,' he muttered. 'May mean some doubling up for you, I'm afraid. Unless you know anyone?' he added, suddenly hopeful. 'A Maths Man?'

I enquired about experience and qualifications, since we'd gone scrupulously into my own in order to arrive at a salary figure.

'Keenness counts for a lot,' he said.

Two days later I caught a train at what was then Amiens Street Station and within minutes was approached by a lean, ageless woman with a distinctively narrow chin. She had guessed who I was, and introduced herself as the teacher of the bottom form. She talked all the way to Portadown, telling me about another preparatory school where she'd taught and which she clearly considered superior to the one we were travelling to. She asked me if I had a cricket bat in my luggage.

'A cricket bat?'

'He promised he'd get a cricket player.'

I shook my head. I had never mastered the game, I confessed. This was probably due to an unnatural exposure to it during a period of my childhood, I began to say, but she wasn't listening.

'He promised,' she whispered. 'I gave him a term's notice and then he promised.'

She looked mournfully out of the carriage window. She couldn't bear another summer term of cricket practices, she whispered, and then repeated this shrilly. Her eyes were wild when she ceased her observation of the waters of the Boyne, over which we happened to be passing. Her face had tightened with emotion, her narrow chin becoming elongated as she struggled with her distress.

'I will not!' she suddenly cried. 'I will not take cricket practices!'

We were alone in the compartment except for a priest who was asleep. He woke briefly, smiled at us, and then returned to his doze.

'I'll not,' the Bottom Form Mistress whispered.

I nodded sympathetically. Perhaps the vacancy for the Maths Man had been filled, I suggested, by someone who knew about the game. Her narrow chin had begun to quiver. I thought she was going to cry.

'I said it to Mother before I left,' she whispered. 'Last thing, in the hall, I said it. Three hours in an icy wind. It's like iron, that ball, if it hits you.'

We had a wait of an hour and a half in Portadown so we walked into the town in search of tea. We couldn't find a café, but a woman in a newsagent's made us some and we drank it standing at the counter. I heard about a boy called Caruth, who aimed the ball at your legs when he threw it to you. We walked back to the railway station. When the train arrived at Killylea a youth in a ramshackle green van was waiting for us.

'Is there another new master?' my companion enquired urgently. 'Did they find another master?'

'Ach, they did of course, miss. They found a great fellow.'

'Has Caruth come back?'

'He did of course, miss. Large as life he is.'

I wedged myself into the back of the van, among suitcases and petrol cans and a sack of something. The despondency of my travelling companion was already infecting me.

★

'Ah, you've met,' the Junior Partner observed as he greeted us in the hall. His manner was even breezier than it had been in the room above the Front Square lavatories. On his home ground, surrounded by the contradictions of all he had claimed for Elm Park, a vigour that hadn't been noticeable before possessed him. It was perhaps necessary in order to live comfortably with the pretence that the establishment was thriving as well as ever it had. The hall was low-ceilinged and elegant, with two finely-proportioned archways, beyond which were an inner hall and the curving incline of a staircase. Trunks and tuck-boxes stood about. On the walls a series of photographs indicated the strength of the school as it once had been.

'Now then, let's see what we can do with you,' the Junior Partner speculated, emanating bonhomie. Moving at speed, he led the way along a corridor, then down uncarpeted stairs. 'Stroke of luck,' he said. 'First class Maths Man.'

A smell of the kitchen developed as we progressed. A clatter of pans and a sharp exchange about burnt peas came from the end of a blue-distempered passage. Some of the blue had flaked away, revealing pink distemper beneath. A door was opened, into what I took to be a coal cellar since the place was in pitch darkness.

'You should be comfy here,' the Junior Partner said. 'Shout if there's anything.'

He unlatched some shutters, explaining that the maids were always pressed at the beginning of term. A light-fitting hung dismally from the centre of the ceiling, cheered by neither bulb nor shade. A mattress, marked with rust, was rolled up on the springs of an iron bed. There was a wooden wash-stand with a white china basin and water-jug on it. The walls were blue, a distemper finish in the same shade as that of the corridor.

'They'll come and sort it out for you,' the Junior Partner promised. 'Shout if they don't.'

The staff-room was next door, he added. A gong would sound for dinner. 'Leave you to get to know one another,' he said.

The staff-room was the same size as my bedroom, the ubiquitous blue distemper flaking on its walls. It contained two tattered armchairs, a table and an empty bookcase. It had greyish linoleum on the floor, and greyish curtains that sagged from the elasticated wire that half-heartedly held them in place. A man was sitting in front of an empty fire-grate.

He was a fat middle-aged man, partially bald, with popping eyes and stained suede shoes. He wore a celluloid collar that had once been white but was now tinged with yellow, as if it had spent some weeks on a sunny window-sill. His checked jacket was torn at one of the pockets; a tie held up his trousers. As soon as he saw me he said:

'You haven't brought a bottle of anything?'

I sat down in the other armchair, apologizing for not having a bottle of something. The Maths Man asked me if I'd brought a wireless and I said I hadn't. He sighed and stared at the empty fire-grate. The food was no better than dirt, he reported. After lunch he'd made his way to the kitchen to have a chat with the cook, who'd given him half a bacon pie to eat. In the kitchen he'd discovered one good thing: every night at dinner the male members of the teaching staff were provided with a bottle of stout each, a tradition that dated back to the founding of the school after the first world war. He asked me if I'd brought a *Reveille* or a *Tit-Bits* with me.

'I'm afraid I haven't.'

He sighed again. For a moment he was silent, his goggle eyes still fixed on the fire-grate. Then he said:

'I wouldn't trust that fellow an inch.'

'Well, he's perhaps —'

'He's dross, actually.'

He'd been resting himself in a local rectory, he went on, when the Junior Partner turned up, announcing he had a vacancy. 'I'll tell you one thing,' the Maths Man said, 'this place is on the skids.'

★

As a bastion of another age, Elm Park had long ago fallen already. What was on the skids in the summer of 1952 was what had replaced it, what had once been a dream — a promise made to one another by two army officers in the trenches more than thirty years ago: to establish, somewhere, a school that was without the humbug of the schools they had known themselves. They found the house, and began with a single boy.

One of them was still there in 1952, almost seventy, bent and thin, with grey hair, and spectacles you didn't notice. Skeletal features were softened by a moustache; when he laughed, which was often, the Old Man did so heartily. He called his dog — a floppy old black-and-white spaniel — Timoshenko, or occasionally Bonzo. Willoughby Weaving he was called himself, a firm clear signature on the fly-leaves of his many

88

books, neatly printed on the single one he had composed himself: a brief sample of his verse.

He didn't write poetry any more and nowadays left the house only to venture as far as the garden. He believed that children should not be physically punished, and in this was in disagreement with the man he had taken on as his partner, a divergence of views that contributed generously to the school's present decline. The twenty-two boys weren't enough. Surrounded by all of them, the Old Man would stroll through the shrubberies of azaleas and rhododendrons, his spaniel bringing up the rear. The older boys talked to him; the younger ones listened. His secret was affection, not so much his for the boys as theirs for him. They gave it unstintingly and trusted him with it, and from it came a discipline he didn't have to demand, and respect he didn't have to bargain for. He was the only adult I have ever met who understood children perfectly.

His most formidable adversary was the Junior Partner's wife, a buxom woman ten years or so older than her husband, the school matron. She and the Old Man had ceased to communicate after a dispute concerning damp football clothes. It was no longer known which of the two had been victorious on this occasion, but it was clear enough that the Junior Partner and his wife had long ago won the continuing war, though whether or not they had won it in time to save the school for themselves seemed increasingly doubtful as that summer advanced. They did their best to keep the place together, hoping to see it through until the Old Man retired and the nonsense about the values of the past and no corporal punishment disappeared with him.

In all this, their staff must have often struck them as a source of neither confidence nor support — a man who'd been resting in a nearby rectory and regretted that he hadn't continued to do so, a woman persecuted by a boy who threw cricket balls at her, a callow youth who was there for the money. By all accounts, our predecessors had been no less prepossessing, especially the dubiously ranked brigadier from Shropshire who questioned the boys about the nightdresses their mothers wore.

Keeping the place together, the Junior Partner rattled about the rooms and corridors, jangling keys or coins, jauntily allocating nicknames to the remaining pupils — Dozer, Oiseau, Scholar Gipsy, Moby Dick. You could see him hoping for the best. As he swung an ancient

lawnmower imperiously about the cricket pitch he, too, had a dream:
boys again crossing the Irish Sea to Winchester and Eton, the numbers
increasing, cricket matches won.

'Dross,' the Maths Man invariably designated the dinner he'd just eaten and would make his way to the kitchen in search of raw eggs, which he cracked into his mouth. Once he persuaded the cook to roast a chicken, and on other occasions to boil saucepans of potatoes, fry herrings, and heat up tripe.

After one such kitchen expedition he confided to me that he'd become interested in a nearby girls' school. He proposed that we should offer our services there as coaches to some of the older girls, who might be in difficulties with their studies. He reported that he'd observed these older girls out for a walk. Worthy of *Tit-Bits*, he said.

So we rode over to the Manor House School one afternoon, having borrowed two bicycles from the maids. It was warm; the distance was several miles and there were hills to climb. 'I think we need a bottle of stout,' the Maths Man suggested, halting at a wayside public house. He ordered chasers of gin and orange, and after that a couple more chasers.

The Maths Man was garrulous for the remainder of the journey, telling me that his ambition was to get out of schoolmastering altogether. He was attracted by the production side of the film business. He had a feeling for films, he confessed, and asked me if I'd ever seen *The Man in Grey*. He said there were companionable girls in the film business, as good as anything you'd find in *Tit-Bits*. A lot of them were on for anything.

Eventually we rode up an avenue as long as the avenue at Elm Park. The wheels of the bicycles squelched over an expanse of gravel in front of an imposing Victorian house. Girls in gymslips eyed us with curiosity.

'Could we see the Head?' the Maths Man enquired of the maid who answered the door.

The maid frowned. She asked if the headmistress was expecting us, and then she asked if we were the men about the fire extinguishers. The bottoms of the Maths Man's trousers were still tucked into his socks.

'The Department of Education,' he said. 'One minute of her time, tell her.'

The maid went away, leaving us standing outside the front door. I suggested that we should mount our bicycles and ride away, that no headmistress would engage tutors for her girls in this manner. The Maths Man didn't respond to this objection. The trouble was, he said, there might be a smell of drink on us. We should have asked the publican for a handful of tea-leaves to chew, or the loan of his toothpaste.

He looked around for the girls who were worthy of *Tit-Bits*. They were probably indoors, he said, taking a bath.

'Yes?' a voice said. It came from a big woman with spectacles, and grey hair in a bun.

The Maths Man held out a hand, which she reluctantly received.

'You're not from the Ministry of Education?'

'No, we're not,' I said.

'I thought —'

'The girl picked that up wrong,' the Maths Man said. 'No, what we were wondering about was grinds for the girls. Extra tuition if a girl had fallen behind. Mathematics, history, geography, religious knowledge. Ten bob an hour.'

'You want to teach my girls?'

'Any girls going in for exams. The bigger girls it would be.'

'But we give tuition here ourselves. That's what we're here for. I have a qualified staff.'

'Would it be best to go inside, miss? If the three of us could sit down at a table —'

'We do not require your assistance here.' The big woman regarded us with distaste. The Maths Man was mouthing at her, his head lowered in the hope that the smell of drink would not reach her. She said she was surprised at us. She closed the door.

We rode away, watched again by the girls in gymslips.

'Have a word with that one,' the Maths Man urged, his eyes goggling as they examined a sulky-looking sixteen-year-old. Ignoring the request, I noticed that he made no effort to engage the girl in conversation himself. 'Dross, that woman was,' he commented when we were again ensconced in the wayside public house. Further distress was drowned in gin and orange.

'You're drunk as an owl, sir,' the boy whose sobriquet was Oiseau delightedly pointed out when we arrived back at Elm Park, his wiry grin floating round in a circle.

The Maths Man left at the end of that term. So did the Bottom Form Mistress. Others came, I left myself. The Old Man retired and went to live in Abingdon. But a second dream was not to be; the numbers declined further, no cricket match was won. Soon after that the chickens moved in at Elm Park.

★

Where are they now, that gallery of children and their mentors, twenty years on? Is podgy Diana a wife and mother? Has Caroline been through the divorce courts? Has a single one of the Junior Partner's nicknames stuck — the Dozer or the Scholar Gipsy, Oiseau or Moby Dick?

The Old Man once wrote from Abingdon, to say that Timoshenko missed the boys. It's safe to guess that Old Pastry's in his heavenly shower-room, that another generation muse and speculate about a colleague over halves of bitter in the Dun Cow, that another Second-in-Command changes into scoutmaster's garb on Fridays. Almost certainly *Staff Laughs* continues to enliven the end of the autumn term. *Apply direct to the Headmaster*, Gabbitas-Thring still advise.

One night in Piccadilly I met the Maths Man. He was scrutinizing the photographs outside a strip-club. He'd given up teaching, he informed me, but I knew he hadn't. I knew he was still sitting in a staff-room somewhere, staring into an empty fire-grate, weaving fantasies about magazine girls. He had spent an hour or two in the strip-club, he confided. 'Dross,' he said.

(1975)

Blockley, Gloucestershire

WHEN I THINK of landscape which is special I find myself back in the County Cork of my childhood. But as a child in Youghal and Skibbereen — poor little towns in those days — I wondered about England: there was a Royal Family, Henry Hall on the wireless, important weddings in the *Daily Sketch*. England spelt elegance, and style and graciousness. It had a capital city so huge that I was assured it would stretch all the way from Skibbereen to Cork City. Occasionally a G.B. car went by, always gleaming, grey or black. If it stopped by the roadside a picnic would take place, a special little kettle placed on a primus stove, sponge cake brought in a tin box from Surrey. Accents were polished, ladies kindly smiled. One of them gave me a fig-roll once.

There was a board-game we played, long before Monopoly. It had to do with train journeys up and down England, all of them beginning at railway stations that had a magic ring: Paddington, Victoria, Waterloo, King's Cross. 'Gloucestershire?' my father said. 'It's a county. Like County Cork or County Clare.' If you were lucky with your dice you might hurry away by G.W.R. to Gloucestershire, while others were stuck en route to Huddersfield or Belper. I imagined a leafy place, nice for picnics, threads of gold among the green. It spread itself out like a tapestry in my mind: nothing was ruined there, no burnt-out houses or smashed castles, no brambles growing through rusty baronial gates as we had in County Cork. The Duke of Gloucester would never have permitted that.

Many years later, when I was in my early twenties but still had not once left Ireland, I came a little closer to Gloucestershire, told about it by the girl I was to marry: about the Slaughters and the Swells, and Adlestrop and Evenlode, in particular about the village of Blockley. That Cotswold world began in marvellous, onion-domed

Sezincote, one of Gloucestershire's stately homes which in 1939 briefly became a haven from German bombs. Afterwards there was a cottage in Blockley itself: Little Manor, a bit overgrown these days, opposite the smart new restaurant that has put the village on the gastronomic map.

For being told about this part of England made me want to visit it, and returning now, I find my childhood vision of an orderly dukedom shattered yet again: it's the hard years of war that come rushing back on a warm July afternoon. Cycling to the grammar school in Chipping Campden, taking the wet batteries to be charged, that's where Miss Tavender lived, that's cruel Fish Hill where you pushed your bike for a mile. The three great houses — Northwick Park and Batsford as well as Sezincote — cannot be as once they were, nor is Sleepy Hollow nor Donkey Lane. And Rock Cottage, where that doubtful prophetess Joanna Southcott spent the last ten years of her life, has been burnt down. But leeks still thrive in the garden that was Sergeant Wall's, and Rose of Sharon in old Mrs Whale's. A pear-tree still decorates a façade in St George's Terrace, the house called Rodneys is still the smartest. Irises and lacy delphiniums prosper, valerian sprouts from the cracks in soft brown walls. Old-fashioned roses are everywhere.

In wartime Blockley there were Italian prisoners of war, laughing while they mended the roads. American soldiers eyed the solitary wives and gave a party for their children, real paste in the sandwiches. 'Aluminium for the war effort!' these same children cried from door to door, taking it in turn to push the pram. They came away with broken saucepans, and between his dozes on a sunny step the village fat boy watched and was amused. He watched as drowsily when the bull ran madly down the long main street, and again when Mrs Jones was dragged the length of it by her husband, unexpectedly home on leave. He watched while villagers brought Mr French a single egg so that he could bake them a cake in Half Crown Cottage. He listened without pleasure while Mr Lunn consoled himself with Bach, or roused himself to warn against the churchyard in the black-out, his thin voice telling of its restless dead.

Blockley nestles, as Broad Campden does, and Shipston-on-Stour. The wolds encase them: lazy undulations, fields guarded by trim stone walls. Patches of sheep whiten the hilly sward, poppies blaze through a field of rye. In the July sunshine the roadside verges are a yard high, yellowing cow-parsley sprinkled with crane's-bill and campion. Elder fills the hedgerows.

In Stow-on-the-Wold you pass down an ancient passage to the Gents, and the hard black oak of door-frames seems tougher than the ubiquitous stone. Above hotels and pubs the wrought-iron signs are motionless on a tranquil afternoon. 'The real McCoy!' an American cyclist proclaims, pausing in one town or another, it doesn't matter which. Tea-rooms are full of shortbread and Bendicks' chocolate mint crisps, part of the scenery.

Domestic pastoral: the Cotswold scene is that, the stone of houses is the stone of the wolds, and Cotswold faces are part of nature too. At dusk, old women in summer dresses make the journey through their village to look at someone else's flowers. At dawn, unshaven itinerants move dourly through the fields from one farm to the next. With passing years, these small conventions remain, even if Northwick Park has become a business school and Blockley's silk mills are bijou residences now. The Gloucestershire voice hasn't altered much, either: on market day in Moreton-in-Marsh it's matter-of-fact and firm, without the lilt that sweetens it further west. Like the countryside it speaks for, its tones are undramatic, as if constantly aware that life owes much to sheep, that least theatrical of animals. While landscape and buildings merge, nobody who lives here is likely to forget that the riches and good sense of wool merchants created the Cotswolds.

When I walk in England I walk in Dartmoor or Derbyshire. I like the English seaside out of season, Budleigh Salterton and Sidmouth and Lyme Regis. But best of all in England there's Gloucestershire to visit and to stroll through, while pheasants rise elegantly from its parklands and rivers modestly make their way. No matter how remote or silent a wood may be there's always a road or a person within reach: I think of Tennyson when I walk in Gloucestershire, the way that runs through the field, two lovers lately wed, an abbot on an ambling pad. I think as well of old Mrs Whale in her lifetime and Sergeant Wall in his, of Albert the footman at Sezincote, Miss Tavender a schoolmistress, and Joanna Southcott. Blockley Brass Band still performs, weather permitting; there are outings to distant Ramsgate. 'Dubious Dog Contest' the sign outside the British Legion hall announces, and I imagine the pink tongues panting on a Saturday afternoon, setters and spaniels that aren't quite the thing,

terriers that should have been Dalmatians. The children of the children
who ate the American soldiers' paste sandwiches self-consciously tug
the leashes. The sun has brought the hollyhocks out.

The countryside is the setting, but people come first: in spite of disturbance and change it is that that continues, and returning now I feel my childhood instinct was not far wrong. In this warm July, or in their wartime years, in snow or sun, the wolds are unique; and their towns and villages perfectly complement them. Crowded with hastening tourists, all three retain their essence: England is unstifled here.

(1981)

A Public-House Man

*A*ny weekday suits, he wrote from Hill Street, w1. *Between 10 a.m. and midday, or if you find it more convenient, between three o'clock and five.*

Shortly after midday he went out to lunch, to the Caprice in the days of his splendour, to the Trattoria Toscana later on. Generally he had not returned by three, but his secretary, Mrs Bartlett, would be there, efficiently holding the fort.

Marchant Smith resembled, almost perfectly, an egg placed on top of a much larger egg. A great domed head, mostly hairless, sloped elegantly down to pick up the line of his shoulders. The ovoid continued, the rotund stomach beneath the striped blue cloth of jacket and waistcoat seeming almost corseted. He was, though stout, neatly made all the way down to his notably small feet.

'I don't see why not,' he said one December morning after we had spoken for no more than twenty minutes in his partitioned office, I seeking employment, he empowered to offer it. Five hundred pounds a year, he then apologetically revealed. It wasn't much, not even in 1959.

Marchant Smith was a double-barrelled name without a hyphen, no doubt created by its present bearer. He was known as Marchant among his friends at his own preference, his given Christian name not being to his liking. Notley's — the advertising agency of which he was the copy chief — was the only one that had held out any hope when I tentatively wrote to a number of them to offer my services. A mammoth concern in St James's might have taken me on if I'd agreed to do six months' selling in Selfridge's and another six months on the road. At J. Walter Thompson's I failed the writing test. Only Notley's welcomed my ignorance of the commercial world and of the craft for which I was presenting myself. On 11 January 1960 I reported there for duty.

'You'll be with Mr Baker,' Marchant Smith said, and led me through a maze of passages. Some of the doors bore visual indications as to the occupants of the rooms, or amusing suggestions as to the qualifications required for working within. From time to time the copy chief paused in his pace to examine these displays, his attention particularly held by a lifesize photograph of two faces behind bars, one bearded, the other grimacing comically beneath a penitentiary-style haircut. 'Droll,' he remarked in weary tones, and without knocking entered the room next door.

'Your trainee, Mr Baker.' He offered me to a raw-faced man in shirtsleeves and red braces, who looked me up and down, evincing what appeared to be mild revulsion.

'What I wanted was an assistant,' he snappishly observed.

'So you shall have, Mr Baker, since you need but turn our friend here into one.'

'I haven't time to turn him into anything.'

'Oh, that we had time, Mr Baker, for all we wish to do! Oh, that we had!'

With that he ambled off, pausing at the door to take his leave of me, inclining his head in a leisurely nod. 'I place you with Mr Baker in the utmost confidence,' he said.

There were broken veins all over Baker's nose and cheeks, which was what gave him the raw look. Crossly, he turned to a girl who was typing and told her to find me a corner somewhere. 'I didn't ask for you,' he said in case I was still under a misapprehension about this.

I learnt later that Marchant Smith had hoped to polish Baker into the kind of copywriter he believed he might become, but that the experiment had dismally failed. Baker was said to have been a bread-van driver, though this may well have been ornamentation on the part of the copy chief in an effort to emphasise his point that he had 'discovered' Baker and 'brought him on' only to receive hostility in return. His error in employing him rankled all the more because he usually sought to fill whatever vacancies cropped up from a somewhat different source: in the 1950s and '60s, Notley's was known in the trade as advertising's 'nest of singing birds' because of the number of aspiring poets it boasted.

A plump young man in a blue blazer was the first of these to intro-duce himself. 'I'm Ted Lucie-Smith,' he said in the room I shared with a waspish typographer, an assembler of point-of-sale display material, and a designer whom the typographer said had aspirations to being a dance-band leader. Lucie-Smith spoke obscurely about contemporary art, at length about himself, and briefly about Clark's Shoes, for which he wrote some of the copy. It wasn't in the least difficult to write advertising copy, he assured me.

I, so far, had written nothing whatsoever. I had been allocated an old Olympia typewriter and a stack of flimsy yellow paper. The two telephones in the room were on my desk, one being a house phone, the other for making outside calls. The aspiring dance-band leader spent a lot of time on the latter, conversing with his wife, whom he addressed as 'chick' or 'doll' to audible sighs of disdain from the typographer. Milky coffee was brought round by a small woman called Nell at ten o'clock every morning, and milky tea at a quarter to three.

'You're getting the hang of things?' Marchant Smith enquired on one of his visits. I said not really, because I hadn't been given any work. 'On that score,' he replied with a sideways inclination of his head, 'you must address yourself to Mr Baker.' Dismissing the subject, he asked me if I had yet met Miss Scott. I shook my head. 'Now *there's* a treat in store for you,' he enthused.

If Marchant Smith felt aggrieved because of the raw-fleshed Baker, he was outraged by Miss Scott. She was a woman of uncertain age with decorated spectacles, who arrived in Hill Street every morning in a taxi, with cage-birds. These had to do with a birdseed account she had charge of, or possibly she had acquired the account through her possession of them. 'My God!' Marchant Smith exclaimed whenever her name was mentioned, and would recount in some detail his most recent observation of her clothing and behaviour. Miss Scott grated on his susceptibilities because she cooed at her budgerigars and endlessly lauded the attractions of Bourne and Hollingsworth, a second-class store she had a hand in advertising. Yet she nourished him as well, fanning a masochism that oiled his wit. Once, when drunk, he spoke of Miss Scott in her bath, describing with sensual delight a nakedness it was most unlikely he had ever witnessed.

Idle at my desk, I watched the birth of point-of-sale material for VP Wine, Kenco coffee, Wolsey underwear, and Britvic fruit and tomato juices. I listened to the whistling of the would-be dance-band leader and the grumbles of the typographer. I envied the poets — Oliver Bernard cleverly purveying the virtues of GKN's screws and fasteners, Peter

Porter doing his best for Bri-nylon, Lucie-Smith inspired by shoes. Later they were joined by Gavin Ewart and Peter Redgrove. 'I have nothing to do,' I muttered whenever Marchant Smith dropped in, and each time he repeated that I must refer this state of affairs to the man whom he sought to irritate by my presence. It became unpleasantly apparent to me that I had been employed for this purpose alone.

Then, most unexpectedly and abruptly, Baker left, taking with him the Courage Beer account and Swan Vesta Matches. 'Your position is greatly altered,' Marchant Smith informed me, and went on to say that I would now be writing all the copy for Canadian Pacific, Sanderson Wallpapers and Fabrics, KLM Royal Dutch Airlines, Sparkletts Soda Siphons, Tube Investments, Wolsey Y-Fronts, Hadrian Paints, Buxted Chickens, *Punch*, and a firm that manufactured brake-linings for buses. 'A tremendous opportunity,' he pointed out.

I failed to seize it. For some reason I found it difficult to appreciate the breakthrough represented by the Y-front or chicken every Sunday. I was far more aware of the fact that from having nothing whatsoever to do I was now grossly overworked. Dozens of pink or blue work-tickets arrived daily on my desk, demanding series after series of double-page spreads, sixty-page catalogues, and mailing shots for travel agents or the painting and decorating trade.

Unnerved by the nature and bulk of these demands, I found myself a constant prey to muddle and misunderstanding. A cocky new account executive who had recently taken over the Tube Investments account phoned me one morning to say that he was lunching with its advertising manager, and requested me to join them afterwards to be briefed personally by this man, a notoriously cantankerous Scot. 'Three o'clock sharp,' the cocky executive ordered. 'I'll be waiting for you on the steps of the Adelphi.' I asked him to be more precise: which particular Adelphi did he have in mind? 'Well, it's not the theatre,' was the best he could do by way of reply, adding somewhat vaguely that the rendezvous in question was on the south side of the Strand.

But when the time came the only Adelphi I could find in that area was a modest Cypriot restaurant, which strictly speaking was in Buckingham Street. Outside this I waited, assuming the two men were lunching within. Three o'clock went by, then a quarter-past, then half-past. In the end I entered the place and found it empty. A waiter told me there was somewhere called the Adelphi Terrace.

'My God, where've you been?' the now-furious executive shouted at me from the steps of this building.

'I'm sorry.'

He'd rung up Marchant Smith, he said, not knowing what else to do. 'He said you were drinking in the Coach and Horses. But when I got through to the bloody place they didn't even know who you were. I can't go rooting copywriters out of public houses, for God's sake!'

'It was earlier that I was in the Coach and Horses actually —'

'I don't care when it bloody was. This man here is doing his bloody nut. He's fit to be bloody tied.'

'I'm sorry —'

'Tell him your mother died. Tell him you were called away to a bedside.'

He swore all the way up to the seventh floor, but by the time we entered the Scotsman's office he had calmed down a little. 'He was held up on jury duty,' he said.

Marchant Smith hugely enjoyed hearing stuff like that: he was the only person I've ever known who chortled. He liked to hear about the ex-commando who was in charge at Canadian Pacific, who was impatient of all those who failed to share his disdain of culture, sensibility and delicacy of expression. And the man at KLM who must in no circumstances be interrupted when he described, yet again, the brass fittings and cushioned seating of his sailing boat. The *Punch* man annually required of some hapless copywriter a lengthy Christmas-card verse retailing his family's activities during the year, details of which were copiously supplied. The representative of a firm that manufactured barrels was a man whose religion forbade him to eat or drink in human company, who had to be shown the way to a lavatory with his lunchtime sandwiches.

'Yes, I quite like that,' Marchant would say when such reports reached him, but when I placed on his desk my latest efforts to promote Canadian Pacific he generally just shook his head. One of these took the form of a reminder that travellers to Canada might like to note that they were following in the footsteps of Leif Erikson. *Come to Canada!* my headline lankly urged.

Scarcely glancing at it, Marchant at once scratched out this injunction. 'Wouldn't you rather say,' he suggested, '*Take a Leif from his Book!*'

He was one of the great copywriters of his time. Growing up with

Picture Post and *Illustrated*, I had become familiar with the guarantee of romance when Knight's Castile Soap was used, and the dissipation of work-place embarrassment with Lifebuoy. 'I even wake up feeling tired,' a worried woman complained, and was informed about Night Starvation. Marchant Smith had been responsible for the Sanatogen advertisements of that same period, those that invariably began, 'Tell me, Doctor . . .' More recently, and with typical simplicity, he had insisted that Top People Take *The Times*.

Struggling to attract visitors to Canadian wildlife, to the wonders of bear and gopher and caribou, I had blankly informed them that *Canada's for You!*

'Wouldn't you rather say,' he gently urged, '*Ever Said Boo to a Caribou?*'

His tongue was his weapon in his snobbishness. He could be blisteringly cruel. But no matter how inept one's own performance, he was always on the side of the copywriters he had given employment to, provided some willingness was shown. He was even occasionally apologetic for not warning them about the mess of ignorance, sharp practice, stupidity and vulgarity he had plunged them into. An army of what he saw as second-rate, lower-middle-class account executives and their assistants — spare-time train-spotters and tropical-fish fanciers, collectors of miniature liqueur bottles, aficionados of tap-dancing — lent inspiration to his scorn when he tired of bathing Miss Scott with it. Sunning himself during summer lunchtimes outside the Coach and Horses, he would entertain his cronies with witticisms he had concocted during his idle morning, while keeping an eye out for the return to Hill Street of the suited figures who so fascinated him. Mr Garwood strode purposefully, as befitted an office manager. Dan Dainty sidled with an underling's deference, head bent to catch a superior's comments. Mr Dibbs came jauntily, Mr Wilkes in a hurry, Fred North uncomfortable with his ulcers. At the approach of a particularly low-browed, shambling youth, grubby-cuffed and famously dense, Marchant's eye would gleam. 'Ah,' he would murmur, 'here comes that wit and bon viveur, Mr Capstick.' The cronies would laugh; and taking this to be a greeting as he went slouching by, the unprepossessing Capstick would cause further mirth by grinning.

Marchant had had his day by the 1960s, and he anticipated retirement by not caring any more, by no longer taking the position he had created for himself seriously. Authority, and power — so sought and so jealously guarded in the business world he had known for so long — were not now necessary as a form of self-protection, since clearly he would be permitted to reach the end of his tenure without the threat of dismissal in old age. He had fixed that, he used to say. His remaining interest was thinking of things to say on his own account, as if to compensate himself for all the phrases he had turned to other people's advantage. When a copywriter, one sunny June morning, remarked on the weather the great ovoid head nodded its agreement. 'Take a letter, Mrs Bartlett,' Marchant roused himself to command. '*Dear God, the very houses . . .*'

He had once been married, an unsuccessful episode in his life, for clearly neither his sensual nor his emotional proclivities lay in that direction. He rarely spoke of his domestic life, but had been noticed at weekends in a public house called the Moscow Arms, near where he lived. Drink had become a way of life with him — a quick one at twelve in the Coach and Horses, Valpolicella lingered over in the Trattoria Toscana, afternoon recourse to the cabinet in his office, again the Coach and Horses, the evening rounded off in the Moscow Arms. Did they wonder about him there: where he went in the daytime, what work he did? Such information often remains secret in public-house society — a veil drawn over what is not revealed, privacy honoured, as it may be, too, in office life. He could have been a butler off duty in the Moscow Arms, or the kind of head waiter who has done no more than pull a chair out since the day his dignity was called upon to rule a dining-room.

'*Quel rendezvous!*' he remarked in the rudimentary, odorous Gents of the Coach and Horses, our shared urinal a blackened concrete wall. And then, as though sooner or later this had to be said: 'You wanted a job, you know. All you have to do is survive.'

He had survived himself. He had wasted himself on breakfast foods and paint and the latest in central heating, when his quick brain, his gift for languages and his probing wit, might have launched him to the top of the English Establishment: he could as easily have belonged in the diplomatic service, the higher reaches of academic life, or succeeded as a newspaper editor. But although at first meeting he seemed the very fabric of that Establishment — his portly form evidence of its rewards, his manner trimmed to the pomposity it approved — he was in fact a cardboard cut-out doing service for reality. Only towards the end of his life — by then affecting a black beret that struck a Gallic and youthful note — did he make the point that he wasn't what his otherwise meticulous dress and butler-like bearing had suggested for so long, that at heart he did not belong to the commerce that claimed him. He was orderly yet a misfit, a saloon-bar character who dreaded seeming an eccentric, a public-house man because his need was an audience.

After his retirement he disappeared into the depths of the Moscow Arms, hobnobbing only occasionally with his old office companions. When news came of his death some wag in the Coach and Horses suggested that '*Tell me, Doctor . . .*' should be inscribed on his gravestone. Better to have recorded that he generously gave employment to the otherwise unemployable, and in his way was as kind as he was cruel.

(1991)

Sarzy

S HE STOOD, SWAYING, with a glass of *vin rosé* in one hand, a packet of Senior Service cigarettes and a crumpled sheaf of yellow typing paper in the other. Sarzy she was introduced as: Frances Sarzano, middle-aged, half Italian, steeped in psychoanalysis, keen on birth signs, grinning and drunk on that Monday afternoon.

'Gemini,' I said when she asked me.

Nothing faltered in her face. There was no sharp intake of breath, no tightening of the fingers on the glass. Scorpio or Capricorn brought all that. Sagittarius turned the grin into a beam of delight.

Her father was a tailor who'd fled to England from the Fascist threat in Northern Italy, settling in Worcester Park. Her parents were now dead; Sarzy lived with a sister in Ewell, but often in the evenings did not return there, preferring to spend the night in the otherwise empty office building, stretched out on one of the account executives' sofas. She was a smallish woman with a large bosom, dressed usually in a navy-blue suit. In the mornings she was spick and span, blouse buttoned, lipstick in place, exuding a determined air of efficiency. In the afternoons she looked as if she'd been exposed to a storm — hair awry, zips unzipped, her yellow typing paper damp with wine.

'What's the matter, love?' Sarzy would ask a lone man, unknown to her, on a barstool. When he replied that nothing was, there'd be the quizzical glance, the sympathetic smile. 'Something's the matter, love.'

Often the man would turn his head away, or open a newspaper he had read already.

'Something's the matter, love,' Sarzy would insist again.

'Nothing's the matter.'

'Are you waiting for your wife?'

'I'm waiting for a friend.'

'When's your birthday, love?'

'Look, I came in here for a quiet drink —'

'Why don't you go home to your wife? Why don't you finish your drink and let me buy you another and then go home to her?'

She loved the thought of men going home to their wives. She loved the thought of other people's happiness, of children born, illness recovered from, duties observed, temptations resisted, the right alliances made when the stars were where they should be. A lifetime of copywriting had not made a cynic of her. She may even have believed what she wrote about Clark's shoes and VP Wine. Happy endings had soaked into her consciousness. Mr Right was really there even if he had not yet approached her personally. The Colgate Ring of Confidence didn't let you down. Dr White came to the rescue on those problem days; there was Yeastvite for energy. Sarzy's saloon-bar conversations with strangers had dialogue in bubbles.

When I first knew her she had just stepped out of her office-bound world to become involved with the remnants of Fitzrovia and Soho. She was still to be seen returning twice in an afternoon from the Curzon Wine Company in Shepherd Market with a tightly-clutched bottle of *vin rosé* or Vouvray. Her hurrying footfall clattered on the uncarpeted back stairs and minutes later she distributed her largesse to anyone who happened to pass the open door of what had, until recently, been a stationery cupboard and was now her office. She frequented the nearby Coach and Horses at lunchtime and in the evenings, but since her discovery of Soho she was more regularly to be found in the Caves de France or the York Minster, or the Swiss pub in Old Compton Street. Dylan Thomas was dead and so was MacLaren Ross, but the Scottish painters, Colquhoun and MacBryde, were still at large, setting a certain Bohemian tone. For his peregrinations through this beer-blurred underworld, Patrick Kavanagh had discarded the battered blue hat that had been so familiar on the streets of Dublin in favour of a cowjammer's cap. Elizabeth Smart had long ago sat down and wept at Grand Central Station, and was trying to forget it. Hangers-on hung on in Jimmy's and the Colony and the Mandrake. Sarzy's generosity to the thirsty was widely enjoyed.

Her particular friend was someone called Daria, whose *bons mots* were regularly quoted; her hero was Winston Churchill because he had won the war against the fascists. She had once, and for years, been in love with a man she talked about, who had written persuasively about steel products, but unfortunately had had a wife and children to go home to. Now, it seemed, she was in love with Colquhoun, but unfortunately he was homosexual. He was there in the agency one afternoon, full of *vin rosé*, dancing with MacBryde. Everyone was invited to watch, the drawing tables in Joyce Peet's big top studio pushed back against the walls, art work and unfinished roughs bundled away, the messenger boy with the Russian name urgently dispatched to the Curzon Wine Company. Sarzy herself hurried off to fetch the more agreeable of the two managing directors, a man she was mistakenly convinced would appreciate Colquhoun and MacBryde. Blue-suited and portly, he arrived, but didn't stay long, muttering as he left that dancing homosexuals were not his thing.

Big Joyce Peet took the floor, and her example was followed by dispatch boys and typists and someone from Accounts. Sarzy kept darting off and returning with account executives who she believed would appreciate the Scotsmen. Then Colquhoun became testy because the dance floor had been invaded. He sulked in a corner and when he became abusive Sarzy said he didn't mean it, but MacBryde said he did. Someone fell into the typographers' camera.

After Colquhoun, Sarzy's affections were claimed by an out-of-work electrician called Charles, whom she almost certainly discovered on a barstool somewhere. Charles was a huge man who rarely spoke and had a fondness for small bottles of high-strength beer. He also had a marital problem, which Sarzy was endeavouring to fix by means of astrological readings and the expertise she had acquired in the field of psychoanalysis through being psychoanalysed herself. Just before five-thirty one evening she was on the house phone, summoning me in hushed tones, as a matter of great urgency, to the disused stationery cupboard. Windowless and dank, it was just spacious enough to accommodate a narrow metal desk, a chair and a filing-cabinet. It also now managed to accommodate Charles, who was lying on the floor in a massive heap, most of him covered with newspaper.

'In case anyone comes in,' Sarzy explained, covering the rest of him.

'Is he all right down there?'

She shook her head. But we must not do anything, she insisted, until everyone had left the building; then we must call an ambulance.

'What's the matter with him?'

'I think he's taken pills.'

Sarzy took pills herself: purple hearts, lifters, anything she could get. But I didn't think she meant pills like that.

'If he has taken something,' I said, 'we shouldn't just sit here.'

'It's only for ten minutes.'

So we waited. And when the departing footfalls on the stairs abated I telephoned 999 and asked for an ambulance. Sarzy poured *vin rosé* for both of us and lifted the newspapers off the man she loved. She smeared on lipstick, powdered her face, and lit a cigarette. She left me with Charles and went downstairs to greet the ambulancemen.

There were two of them, and a stretcher, which had to be left outside because there wasn't room for it in the stationery cupboard. There wasn't room for the ambulancemen either. We were touching one another as we stood there. 'What's up with him?' the taller man asked me. I said I didn't know.

The sheets of newspaper were still scattered on the floor. A one-bar electric fire which Sarzy had borrowed to keep Charles warm while he lay on the concrete floor had begun to singe the bottoms of his trousers. An empty Vouvray bottle was on its side in a corner.

'Hey, you!' the taller of the ambulancemen shouted into Charles's face. 'What's the matter with you?'

'He was threatening to take pills,' Sarzy said. 'I think he did in the end.'

'What kind of pills?'

She shook her head. He'd had a lot of trouble, she said, Pisces married to a Capricorn.

Charles's pockets were searched, but no pills were found. The taller ambulanceman roughly prodded his neck, then smacked his cheeks. Charles groaned.

'He's drunk,' the smaller man concluded furiously, red in the face. He was quivering with rage. All over London there were people dying, he said; there were people in distress, people in accidents, people who needed to be conveyed to hospitals. Both men, having crouched over Charles for several minutes, were upright again. The taller one was glancing distastefully about him — at the sheets of newspaper, the empty bottle in the corner and the partially full one on the metal desk, the two glasses beside it. There was a smell of burning. A curl of smoke was rising from one of Charles's turn-ups.

'Did you think to alert a fire brigade while you were at it?' the smaller man enquired nastily. I turned off the electric fire and said I was sorry. The other ambulanceman sniffed.

'What's the matter, love?' Sarzy asked him.

'This turkey'll sleep it off is what the matter is. Next time just leave him to get on with it.'

Sarzy offered the men cigarettes. 'Please wait a moment,' she said when the gesture was ignored.

'For what, madam?'

'I'll fetch two more glasses.'

The ambulancemen didn't speak again. They picked up their stretcher and went. On the floor Charles began to snore.

Half an hour later when I looked in at the Coach and Horses he was standing at the bar. Sarzy was rooting in her handbag for something to pay for his extra-strength beer with.

Such lame ducks were her stock-in-trade — the sacked, the dodgy, the deadbeats of the Caves de France, the suicidal. When they didn't conveniently surface she created them: in a matter of minutes she could turn a carefree stranger into a mass of inhibitions. Her head would roll a little to one side, her eyes acquire a shared-confidence look. Bubbling with encouragement, everything about her willed a confession of father-fear or mother-fixation, or revelations of destructive toilet training. Beneath a polished surface she often discerned greed or ruthlessness, even a whiff of evil. Others could do no wrong. 'A nice one,' she would say about a newly arrived young executive whom she had met for a moment in the lift. There was rarely a reason why some were good and others distrusted as future harbingers of grief or pain.

The agency's founder, Notley, was one of the good. Attributes of decency, straight dealing and honesty were affectionately applauded, a forthright Cockney manner endearingly dwelt upon. That the three former qualities were not always readily discernible to the less perceptive hardly came into it. Just as the much-quoted Daria was designated a wit even if her *bons mots* were not what the expression implies, so Notley's moral rectitude — sharing rank with that of angels and bishops — was stated as a fact.

'Do something for me,' Sarzy requested humbly when Notley lay dying. 'Light a candle for him.'

Because I was Irish she insisted on assuming I was a Catholic in spite of my frequent denials.

'Please,' she begged. 'On your way home light a candle.'

I began to explain, yet again, that I didn't have access to miraculous intervention through candles.

'Please. That church in Farm Street, next to the little brown pub.'

The shared-confidence smile was there, the dishevelled head cocked challengingly to one side. She would sleep tonight, she reminded me, if I lit a last candle for Notley. It would take only a few minutes. It was what any good man would want. Then she thought of something else and said:

'Light one for Tommy Kenyon too.'

Tommy Kenyon was not numbered among the chosen. But because he was in hospital recovering from something to do with the walls of his stomach, it wouldn't be fair — it wouldn't be right — that a candle shouldn't burn for him also.

Notley died. Tommy Kenyon was back in the office within a week, on a diet of milk drinks and slop. Although I hadn't lit anything for either of them, and constantly said so. Sarzy always believed I had and that in doing so had offered up the candles carelessly, muddling them in some way. During the rest of the time I knew her she tended to bring that up.

Somewhere she found a dead cat and insisted that it was not entirely lifeless. She wandered from office to office with the remains of the creature wrapped in a duster, in search of someone who knew about feline diseases. She mentioned candles again, but this time I refused more firmly.

In the end they let her go. She had taken to interrupting afternoon meetings to enquire of the agency's clients what the matter was and may even have shown the dead cat to a couple of them. Men who manufacture wallpaper paste or nylon yarn do not take kindly to such interruptions, so Sarzy — after a vast number of years in the service of their products — was pensioned off.

Everyone missed her. Everyone said her heart had been in the right place: her persistence and her wild probings of other people's psyche had all to do with that. She suffered fools gladly, and didn't mind bores. She bewildered the conventional and the dull — two descriptions she would not have permitted herself to use. She was a woman about whom no ill was spoken, even by those whom she considered her enemies. Her tiresomeness was always forgiven: something about her made that seem natural.

Life in Ewell wasn't for her, people said; she would not survive there. But she did. She survived for another ten years, before the *vin rosé* and the Vouvray belatedly took a toll. There was a stroke, and then she died in a hospital for incurables.

(1991)

Assia

THE SIXTIES IN London had the flavour of a dream. After the drabness of the previous decade, in which nothing more exciting happened than Ban-the-Bomb marches, the Suez fiasco and a dog propelled into space, all of a sudden there was the razzmatazz of Carnaby Street and the E-Type Jag, and smart Mary Quant bringing fashion they could afford to shopgirls and typists. Flower people ran barefoot in the park, James Bond pushed aside the fuddy-duddy heroes who still trailed a Bulldog Drummond sense of decency and a stiff upper lip. Cannabis was in, LSD if you were daring. Sex set up its stall. *Jesus Christ is alive and well,* the graffiti said, *and working on a less ambitious project.*

Fantasy arrived in London in the 1960s. 'It's fantastic!' was the cry as wives were swapped at parties and there was dancing without steps. Fans ruled London's football terraces, tuneful with 'Here we go!' More fans than ever before mobbed the entertainment idols. Popular music acquired significance, and the record companies a very great deal of money. Going topless was all the rage.

So were rude words on chat shows, doing your own thing, and youth. Jack Kennedy, ikon of the young at heart, became President of the United States. Suave Dr Stephen Ward, osteopath and sexual provider, amassed a stable of nubile lovelies for the delectation of the powerful and the good.

In 1962 a young man in a lounge bar won a wager of a shilling by kissing on the lips a girl who was a stranger to him: she'd have slapped his face in the nineteen fifties, and taken him to court in the nineties. But in the sixties — mid-century breathing space between the World Wars and Aids — everybody laughed and anything went. 'Yeah! Yeah! Yeah!' sang the Beatles, and all over London there were poets — barrow poets and Putney poets and Hampstead poets, poets in movements and in groups, poets homing in from the antipodes and from Africa, from India and Ireland and Wales and Scotland, beat poets, obscure poets, sober poets, drunken poets, good, bad and indifferent poets. All of them were reading aloud, sonorously or quietly, in drill-halls or cold upper rooms.

With one of them came Assia, tall and beautiful, her features reminiscent of Sophia Loren in a tranquil moment. When she spoke it was huskily, her tone aristocratic, its perfect English modulations belying a background of muddled nationality. Of Russian extraction — though reports of this from Assia herself varied — she had arrived in England via Israel and Canada. Her poet was David Wevill, a newly acquired husband with a look of the young Gary Cooper and sounding like him too — a whispering Canadian drawl reluctantly emerging from the poetic reverie that seemed always to possess him. Charming, attractive, unobtrusive, they were Scott Fitzgerald people sixties-style, their innocence brushed over with sophistication, their devotion to one another taken for granted.

Telling the story of their meeting, and their subsequent marriage, Assia's recollection of detail varied also: the encounter on an ocean voyage was sometimes an encounter on a train or in a café. But discrepancies never mattered much: what was consistent was that two strangers fell in love, that the wedding was romantically impulsive, that film-star lookalikes can belong together as totally as other people.

Assia liked getting married, but was vague about how many times she actually had been. Once, walking past Moyses Stevens the flower shop, then in Berkeley Square, she said: 'Let's try this,' and a moment later was introducing herself as someone's secretary — which she was not — and ordering flowers in his name.

Glancing over the vast array of delphiniums and freesias and carnations, she arranged for a dozen and a half red roses to be dispatched immediately to her declared employer's wife. Her sudden inspiration pleased her enormously. On the pavement outside, among hurrying mini-skirts and warm-complexioned executives jostling for after-lunch taxis, she said:

'The poor woman's pregnant.'

Sending roses, or anything that might bring comfort, to a pregnant wife was, apparently, not this husband's style, a man you had to nudge if you were after some modest courtesy.

'In error I married him once,' Assia said.

But if Assia made mistakes she also had vision. You couldn't buy a decent ice-cream in London, she rightly pointed out, and suggested that a simple co-operative venture would rectify the situation and solve the acute pecuniary problems currently experienced by most of the people she knew. All that was necessary were a refrigerator, which could be purchased in a junk yard, an old bread van, various ingredients, an Italian recipe book, and a little practice. The produce would be conveyed about the suburbs of Primrose Hill and Hampstead Heath on warm Saturday afternoons, welcomed by the local children. She herself would dispense the largesse at economical prices, requiring only a wooden spoon and a supply of cones. She saw herself splendid in white, her Saturday arrival in the suburbs a cause for celebration among delighted children. But no one knew of a junk yard with abandoned refrigerators for sale, or where an ice-cream recipe book might be obtained, and no one possessed an old bread van. 'We'd have made our fortune,' Assia declared sadly but philosophically.

In much the same way, while strolling about the lunchtime streets or esconced in the corner of a bar, she would outline the complicated plot of a novel that someone else might care to write. What she related never sounded quite like fiction, more a sleight of hand involving real people and the real world. Relating her plots, fantasy and fact flowed over one another, confusing the convoluted story she was attempting to communicate, but enriching the actuality of Assia herself. In all this she managed never to sound dotty, well aware that dotty girls are not attractive. Being attractive was important to her.

She smoked but did not drink. Coca-Cola was what she asked for, and always with an apologetic smile. Some people distrusted that smile, were made uneasy by this big-limbed girl with the *femme fatale* voice and elegant dress sense. Yet Assia seemed less a predator than a notably happy wife: in one another's company, both she and David Wevill continued to exude the good fortune that had brought them together. When their sudden break-up came it sounded like news misreported, a fate that belonged to two other people. And ironically, as related by Assia herself, the news was not without inaccuracies.

She reported that she and her husband, advertising in the *Evening Standard* a table for sale, met — through their efforts to sell it —

David Wevill's fellow-poets Ted Hughes and Sylvia Plath, who were at that time man and wife. According to one at least of Sylvia Plath's biographers, what was advertised was a flat. But a table formed a more interesting heart to the story Assia told, the fingers of the poets passing lightly over its surface as value and age were assessed. The biographer's version of this encounter is no doubt the correct one: tables, in 1962, were rarely advertised in the *Evening Standard*.

'Heavens, the coincidence of it!' Assia exclaimed in genuine wonderment. 'All three of them being poets!'

Her tone of voice made her the outsider: she had no lines to offer in that charmed poetic circle. One day she might have the right to be there, but for the moment she possessed little more than beauty and an imagination she could not properly make work for her. As with the rich, she was fond of saying, when you were beautiful you never knew why people liked you. Being loved for herself alone was what she hoped for when she tried to sell ice-cream.

'We were invited for the weekend,' she reported, and then there was a description of the train journey, the landscape, the tranquillity of a Devon farmhouse. The occasion of this fateful weekend was recalled in Grosvenor Square, on a warm June afternoon. Office workers chewed their sandwiches or just lay about. Perched on a huge Dennis lawnmower, a man was cutting the grass.

'On the Saturday evening I made a salad in their kitchen,' Assia said, and described a scene in which her host had found her doing so, and how they'd talked, and how she'd been attracted by him.

'I think I'll send him this.' As she spoke, she bent down and picked up a blade of newly chopped grass. She held it delicately between a patiently manicured thumb and forefinger. She said:

'Just by itself.'

'D'you think that's a good idea?'

'Not really.'

Later she addressed an envelope, and dropped into it her blade of grass. It didn't seem like a brazen action, more like a bid to enter that charmed circle by playing with fire for the sake of it. Within three days, I was told — since I was now the confidant in all this — that an envelope had come back: beside the scrap of London grass lay one from Devon. I wasn't shown it; I didn't know if what was claimed was true. It sounded unlikely, a romantic novelist's device clumsily deployed to stoke up the plot. But some weeks later Assia confided:

'We met for tea.'

The Beatles might have made a song of it: tired waitresses among the aspidistras while a beautiful woman searched yet again for marital perfection. That she had already found it, as everyone thought, was too ordinary and old-fashioned for the bright new sixties, in which doing your own thing was still what mattered most. But the times were changing even as they occurred. When Lee Harvey Oswald did his thing it wasn't so good. Nor when Brady and Hindley did theirs. Stephen Ward's loveliest lovely was in gaol, the osteopath himself was dead. Tut-tutting over bad taste in some Northern schoolroom, Mrs Mary Whitehouse was planning to clean up those parts of the permissive society that showed. As London boasted of being the fashion centre of the world, the feminists were grimly burning their bras. The seeds of Europe's Vietnam were germinating in Belfast and Derry. With half the decade to go yet, the fun fair was sleazy at the edges.

'Tea!' Assia said. 'Imagine it!'

Since the whole episode — the table for sale, the salad preparation, the eccentric love tokens — was already imbued with the wild instability of a dream, nothing now seemed impossible. Whether the recollected minutiae of the teatime rendezvous were exact, or tinted with a personal emphasis, was irrelevant. Liars lie in order to obscure; Assia exaggerated only in the interests of what she saw as a greater veracity and, as her voice continued, doubts slipped away. Clearly, some part of this was not invented, but how the truth and the liberties taken with it were arranged I did not then know.

All that was luminously apparent was that Assia already saw herself as the Other Woman, and already she spoke of Sylvia Plath as an Other Woman might be expected to: 'a brisk, hard, magazine-editor kind of American'. This assessment was considerably at odds with the opinions of those who knew Sylvia Plath well, but in making the statement Assia spoke from the rôle she had allocated to herself, her judgement swamped by prejudice and the fear of being considered hard herself. Then, unexpectedly, reality called everyone to attention: for reasons that were mysterious and have remained so since, Sylvia Plath killed herself.

A long time later, after Assia's only child was born, she telephoned me and we met in the lounge of a bar near Waterloo. Chain-smoking and still drinking only Coca-Cola, she continued the history of her life: in the interim since last we'd conversed she had been, as she put it, 'far out into the night'. Her marriage to David Wevill was over. She was alone with her child in a flat in Primrose Hill. Bleakly shadowed by the extravagance and vigour of her past, this mundane existence did not sound tranquil.

'What would you say if I got married again?' she suggested.

'Nothing very encouraging, Assia.'

She mentioned the Heather Jenner agency, a well known marriage bureau in Bond Street, fashionable at the time. Quite seriously, she suggested filling in various forms and ending up with a widower in the country somewhere. She'd had enough of poets. With her eyes half closed against the stream of smoke from her cigarette, she even referred to a cottage garden, with lupins and fuchsia, and wistaria round the porch. She gave the impression that she meant every word of it.

'It's not a good idea, Assia.'

'I want to take my child away from Primrose Hill.'

'There are less complicated ways of doing that.'

'I think I might make a farmer happy.'

There was the lavish smile. The freckles on the bridge of her nose were disturbed by a wrinkle that came and went. Nowhere in her features was there any sign that she felt sorry for herself. Her eyes were full of yet another Alice-in-Wonderland future: an elderly, kindly man in gaiters, touches of white in his hair, she herself stirring milk in a saucepan, her child in its cot by an open fire. She had no doubt she could make it happen.

She went on talking about that with increased conviction. For the first time she called herself a displaced person, tumbled about by circumstances, and war; for the first time she confessed she had created the woman she seemed to be, teaching herself an upper-class English voice and making the most of her looks, using them as a stepping stone whenever the chance offered. She spoke of her Russian blood, of childhood in Israel, and then being shipped away to Canada and the first of her marriages. The hours she talked through that night near Waterloo Station were like hours spent in a cinema. Images were

left vividly behind, flights of fancy mingled with undecorated verities. Outside, on a cold night, she turned up the collar of a smart tweed coat and for a single instant seemed weary, as though she'd talked too long and said too much. Defeat, suddenly there, faintly distorted her features, dragging at the corners of her mouth.

'Actually I'm afraid,' she murmured, before she smiled again and went away.

A month or so later Assia killed her child and then herself.

(1985)

Out of Season

O N A MONDAY morning in February not much was happening in Sussex by the sea, and nothing had changed. In the chilliness the pale cliffs of the South Coast still gleamed with an elegance that wasn't reflected in the architecture of pavilion and hotel: along miles of promenade bow-windows were still the rage, and clean cream paint, and onion domes squatting importantly, confident of their grandeur. Grey-brown waves snarled beneath the deserted piers, old men walked alone. Wallpaper of rich red flock was being eased from the walls of a palm-court lounge, to be replaced with something similar for the coming season. 'Ridiculous,' murmured the Irish workman whose task it was. 'A total waste.' In ice-cream parlours chromium chairs were stacked on tables; novelty sausages, made of rock, gathered a dust in the windows of closed humbug shoppes. *Lady seeks small flat, not on a hill*, a postcard read in the window of a tobacconist. *Are we being visited by humans from outer space?* another enquired. *Do Flying Saucers exist? What do they want?*

Elsewhere, winter functions were more boldly heralded. Dale Martin Promotions were billed to bring wrestling to the Pavilion, Mal Kirk versus Majid Ackra, Don Vines and Carlos Moll. *Madame Butterfly* was on the way, and a lecture (with slides) about the Caravan Cities of the Desert. There were forthcoming Coffee Mornings, meetings of Floral Groups and the Spice of Life Club, the Civil Service Pensioners, the East Sussex Alsatian Training Club. *The Erotic Urge* was showing at a cinema. 'French girls at their kinkiest,' promised the poster. Bingo was everywhere. Leisurely pedestrians nodded their heads, reading slowly. Bob Miller and the Millermen were shortly due: the young were catered for, but the young weren't much around. On a Monday morning in February the seaside belonged to the old, to people no longer in a hurry. *A Walking Stick Makes A Good Companion*, a sign said.

Head waiters yawned that morning over the stubs of their ciga-

rettes, pondering with a bored eye the menus of the day. Vegetable
Soup and Curried Duck, Roast Lamb, Mint Sauce, Veal à la Romaine,
Garden Peas, Brussels Sprouts, Potatoes roasted or sauté, boiled or à la
Duchesse, Creamed Tapioca, Curate's Pudding, Rice and Apple Souf-
flé, Cheese and Biscuits, Coffee extra. In a deserted bar a commercial
traveller read, framed in gilt, a 'Chart of Good and Bad Times'. Soon,
he learnt, it would be a favourable period in which to buy stocks and
to corner lots, after which there might again be times of panic, and hard
years and low prices. Many had profited from the prophecies, so the chart
claimed, since first they were published, in 1872, by George Tritch of
Denver, Colorado. Unimpressed, the traveller sighed and moved away.
He'd been selling patent medicines, he told me, for twenty-two years:
there was a nice steady response all along the Coast. 'Old timers,' he
said. 'They like their pills.'

In the writing lounge of an immense, blue-carpeted hotel men in
business suits sat in conference. They smoked cigarettes and pipes in
that hot room, their coffee cups were empty. Harsh winter sunlight fell
on their faces and on the red baize of their conference table. They were
men in the car-battery business; they spoke in turn, reporting a year's
sales, some of them a little uneasily. Each wore a metallic badge on his
left lapel, white letters on a red ground, the name of the bearer and the
area he represented. R.T. Atkins, of Horwich, went into greater detail
than the others. He held up two sheets of graphs and explained them.
'There's a specific and individual history behind every sale,' he said. 'In
this day and age close study pays dividends.' The eyes of some of his
colleagues closed; others sighed, looking out at the light blue sky. 'My
figures bear me out, I think,' continued R.T. Atkins. 'This pattern's as
clear as water.' He smiled beneath a small moustache. Two more of his
colleagues slept.

Outside, the cream and green Southdown buses crept along the
coast road, from Worthing to Eastbourne and far beyond it, inland to
little towns at peace in February. High on their hill, the girls of Roedean
continued their expensive routine, perhaps lifting their eyes in a moment
of tedium to gaze out at the sea that everyone else, visitor and resident,
old and young, must occasionally gaze at too — the sea that made the
history of the island they all shared. Miles away, at Battle Abbey, other
girls continued also, knowing that few visitors would today roam the
grounds of their school in search of the spot where Harold died. And

on the hard, tourist-worn earth of Hastings Castle two lovers strolled, seeking a privacy that only winter brings in that famous place.

The old and the retired: in this out-of-season vacuum they made more sense than travelling salesmen or men in the battery business, or schoolgirls, or lovers. They belonged, and seaside Sussex belonged to them. Wrapped up well, for in an increasingly bitter wind the sun was only a mockery, they walked with care the long promenades or sat in their guest-house conservatories, listening to the wireless. 'If you're driving an articulated vehicle,' chirped Jimmy Young, 'do please be ever so ever so jolly well careful.'

Husbands and wives picked their way to the shops with a string bag each, to share the load. Companions met for morning coffee in the Bondolfi Café in Eastbourne, and in Bognor Regis too, and Littlehampton and Rustington, in Worthing, Hove and Hastings, in Middleton-by-the-Sea, and Shoreham and Bexhill, and St Leonards and Rottingdean. In snug public houses conversations flourished, over stout and bitter and green chartreuse. In a seafront shelter an ancient voice approved the Duke of Edinburgh. 'And the Prince of course, his father's son. So nicely mannered: royal stock, royal stock.' He sat alone, upright and thin, his eyes through spectacles staring at the sea, murmuring his private conversation.

'We're used to invasion,' a retired dentist less privately said in Eastbourne. 'The Normans came in off that sea, and the Saxons before them. D'you follow me, sir? South Saxons, Sud Seaxe, Sussex. D'you see, sir? It's different now.' The new invaders come armed with money, to spend it happily on solid English fare in this most English part of England, on Babycham and beer, iced gin and orange, whisky macs and vodka gimlets, long sticks of rock, holiday gifts and holiday reminders. *George!!* cries the message on an ashtray. *George, George, you're smoking too much!* Some George at home will receive it with a smile, glad that he was not forgotten. Mugs, breezily inscribed *Lily's False Teeth* or *Nan's Choppers*, await the gay good mood of holidaytime. *Life*, a decorated tea-strainer giggles, *is one long strain*. The locals in winter pass them all by, preferring to note the dates of promised Whist Drives and Olde Tyme Dancing, symphony concerts, and the new Dale Martin Promotions.

That day was the eighty-second birthday of a lady whose greatest pleasure now was to play the pins in a pink cafeteria. There, in

Bexhill-on-Sea, a resort whose crest bears the simple legend *Sol et Salubritas*, she operated with skill a fruit machine containing a game of chance called Safari. 'Kick the bloody thing,' her cold-faced husband called across a waste of unoccupied tables. 'Kick it, Dorothy, it never works.' He wished she'd leave the machines alone, he confided to me: they weren't well off: she always lost. 'Still, at our age something has to keep you going. The television's a load of muck.' He shook his head and didn't notice when I spoke. I went to watch her at play and without lowering her voice she explained that she didn't let him see when the machine worked in her favour, in case he'd want the money. She smiled: this small deception was what really kept her going. Coins spluttered out. 'I've turned his deaf-aid off,' she said, disguising a movement of her hands, winking her delight: she'd been a flirt in her time.

In a smarter place — the long, glass bar of a hotel — an old man seemed to be the late C. Aubrey Smith. White-haired and cleanly dressed in pale brown corduroy, he had his own bottle of Harvey's Bank sherry brought from behind the bar every morning to share with whatever visitor he might have. There was dignity in his conversation even though, as he himself pointed out, he was not sober. 'Terrible town for fogies,' he said. 'Shocking time of year. Terrible, the South Coast, for fogies.' His mind reverted; he told me yachting stories; he reminisced about the war. A long time ago now he had achieved distinction in the Navy. His speech was slightly slurred, contrasting sharply with his tidy appearance. 'I like my sherry in the morning,' he confessed, 'and Teacher's later on. It sees me through.' From where we stood we could see the sea and people passing, quite close by, on the promenade. I watched a child walking on a wall. 'We're not entirely without the young,' the old man said. 'The young grow up and the old grow older: we have a lot in common.' He issued a short roar of laughter and poured more sherry.

His wife, he said, had died nine years ago; they'd had no children. Her death, though anticipated, had been a shock and after it he'd moved to this big hotel, with its Harvey's Bank in the morning and Teacher's later on. A woman in the town, an old friend of his wife's, did a bit of shopping for him, for often when the weather was chilly he didn't much care for going out. She'd been married too, he said; she tried to keep busy now because her husband had been alive not all that long ago; they were in the same boat in a way. The conversation changed, but in time the woman he spoke of came in, with a tube of toothpaste for him in a paper bag. She was younger, but not all that much younger, fragile and very thin, her lips and fingernails meticulously painted. 'It ain't going to rain no more, no more,' the old man suddenly sang, as though her presence demanded this eccentric gesture. She laughed, throwing her head back, and he laughed too. 'I was reminding our friend,' he said, 'that we have a thing or two in common with the very young: we need looking after, for a start.' He looked at me and repeated, as though in love with the phrase: 'The young grow up and the old grow older.' More laughter followed and I left them in that merry mood, happy with one another, missing two other people.

Later on, through the cold afternoon, a funeral moved. Another old woman nudged her husband: he took his hat off. 'Shh,' a man whispered to his dog. They stood quite still, three people and a dog, and it seemed in that moment that in these seaside towns, among the elderly and the retired, courtesy and gentleness were still part of the condition of life. There was a tetchiness too, but it was tetchiness without a bitter lining, an anger that was modest. On the streets the old did not jostle, doors were held open for ladies going first, there was all the time in the world to listen to what was being said. The funeral passed on and the people moved again, with death on their minds maybe, or maybe not. In a church not far away a service of Compline began.

No one said it, but everyone was waiting for summer. Their haunts would be taken over then, but the holidaymakers were an entertainment in themselves, to watch and talk about. Some vicarious pleasure might even be derived from all the snazziness of the contemporary young and middle-aged in action, from images of passionate dancing in the great pavilions and ballrooms, and crowds in the early morning. But the summer was still a long way away, and in the meantime there were only a few winter visitors, the small following drawn by a table-tennis or a bridge tournament, the conferences of politicians and businessmen. Associations of professional women might come for a day or two to talk about being women and professional. Advertising executives would arrive with their solemn briefcases, and out-of-term headmasters, members of the Incorporated Association of Preparatory Schools, and marketing men and Work Study groups, and trade unions, and members of the Magic Circle, and vintners and opticians and land-scape gardeners.

On this February day the men of the car-battery industry finished their discussions in the blue-carpeted hotel and ate Cotelettes de Porc à la Robert. The residents, sitting silently at their separate tables, eyed them familiarly, as was, they felt, their right. The men still wore their name-badges; R.T. Atkins, of Horwich, was talking about a cat. His voice carried to all his companions and to others as well. He'd been sitting one Sunday afternoon in the house of his brother-in-law in Croydon, with the cat on his lap. Suddenly, to his amazement and the amazement of his brother-in-law, the cat had caught him by the end of the thumb and wouldn't let go. The marks were still there. A.K. Blackledge, W. Evans, C.H. Newell, T.J.S. Martin and a man whose badge was on upside down examined the thumb, passing it on from one to another. One of them remarked that cats were notorious for the sharpness of their teeth. R.T. Atkins agreed with that. It was an extraordinary thing to have happened; the cat had held on from half-past eight until almost midnight; a veterinary surgeon had been summoned in the end. 'Like something you'd read about,' said the man whose badge was upside down, 'in the Guinness Book of Records.' At another table two of the battery men quietly laughed. 'I've a couple of addresses in this town,' one of them confided. 'Topless clubs. D'you feel in the mood?' They moved from the dining-room. The residents waited until the others had left also before making, in a body, for the television lounge. 'Are they the boilermen's union?' a neat lady in grey asked her younger companion and the companion replied that grown men should have more sense, no matter who they were.

The streets were quiet that night. Chez Maurice, famous for tournedos Masséna, was almost empty. Skinheads conversed in the gloom of a café, their fingers on the legs of girls; a late commuter strode purposefully from the railway station. Sniffing the salty air, two clergymen with walking-sticks spoke of St Paul. Seagulls cried. There was no one on the front.

In a panelled saloon bar, estate agents talked politics with local bankmen, easily agreeing that Harold Wilson, operating from within the Conservative Party, could be the Prime Minister of the century. They were friendly people. It was the wrong time of year to see the Coast, they told me, not that they themselves didn't appreciate the peace. Mind you, Brighton was lively all year round, and Hastings too in a way. But they preferred the seasonal contrast; they wouldn't live anywhere else. There were chaps, actually, who'd spent their lives saving up in order to retire to the seaside of Sussex, just for the briny and the seasonal contrast. Old dads and their biddies: you couldn't miss them in the daytime, but by now they were probably all in bed.

In the bar of the blue-carpeted hotel one of the battery men remained. It was R.T. Atkins, who by the sound of things had driven his companions elsewhere. A tomcat in Croydon, he was telling the barman, had once attacked his thumb. He told me too, saying that earlier he'd been telling his colleagues about it. The cat had been put down, he said, and then he went away.

The barman appeared to be in a sulk. 'We had a crowd of builders at the weekend,' he said. 'The worst lot ever.' He shook his head; he looked as if he couldn't smile. Two builders for a joke had thrown two others into the sea and there'd been trouble, also, in the female staff quarters.

It was nice in winter, the barman said, except when the conferences arrived. You had a nice day, pouring sherry and Guinness, and a nip of brandy in the evening. They were decent people who came in and had a chat and a smoke and weren't a nuisance. Who wanted to hear, for heaven's sake, about some animal in Croydon? Even the season was better than that; you knew where you were with the season.

The man who earlier had claimed to have useful addresses in the town entered the bar with a colleague. 'Oh, damn hell,' muttered the barman.

'God-forsaken bloody area,' shouted the man with the addresses. 'Isn't there anything alive in this town, for the sake of Christ?'

His friend ordered drinks, and the barman, pouring them, said there wasn't much doing in wintertime. Brighton was more the place.

'I had the addresses of two joints. Topless. You know. I had firm addresses but the taximan said they didn't exist.'

'They're places in Grimsby, Jack,' his friend reminded him with a trace of weariness in his voice. 'We've established that if nothing else.'

The man with the addresses stared in silence at the barman, his lower lip protruding. 'You're a local,' he said at length. 'Doesn't anything ever happen on this bloody coast? We've been to four towns tonight. We're bloody frozen.' The barman rinsed a glass. Nothing much happened, he patiently repeated. Bob Miller and the Millermen were due next week, but apart from that it was naturally quiet in winter. It was right

and proper, the barman suddenly said with heat; you couldn't expect anything else. It was in the nature of things.

The other man began to argue. Still listening to him, I went away. Tomorrow it would be the same. The old would go on the same walks. They would sit in the same corners. The sea would snarl beneath the piers, and from Bognor Regis to Hastings morning coffee would be taken and the world news discussed at leisure. By the Sussex seaside the old would grow older in the wintry sun, enjoying the seasonal contrast. They would live their pleasant life, while men of business absurdly came and went, and the young grew up.

(1970)

To Persia in the Old Days

'YOU ARE REALLY lonely,' the anaesthetist remarks on the Orient Express, 'when you find yourself reading your toothpaste tube.' He pauses and then elaborates, adding that in Ethiopia a bout of homesickness had once been comforted by the address on a carton of Sterilised Plain Lint Finger Dressings. Boots, Nottingham, England, had had a lovely ring about it.

In Voiture 89 there are an Italian couple in suede overcoats, two American women, a Frenchman with a ciné-camera, and other travellers who so far have only briefly appeared. I share my sleeping compartment with the anaesthetist, and on the second night he opens the communicating doors to the next compartment and invites me to join him and his friends for dinner.

His friends are a colonic surgeon and his wife, who appears to run a launderette. They have a Fortnum and Mason's hamper. I have sandwiches and a bottle of whisky. There is no dining-car on the Orient Express and the coffee-car doesn't come on until we cross the Turkish border in two days' time. I trade some of my whisky for slices of duck.

In the corridor the two American women chatter. I have encountered them already: one is big, loosely clothed, with spectacles; the other is kittenish and fluffy. They belong in the compartment on the other side of ours, the anaesthetist has gloomily divulged: he has taken against these women.

The hands of the colonic surgeon shake as he spreads Russian salad on a Bath Oliver. He notices me observing this and remarks that a stomach surgeon's hands can shake quite safely, even a brain surgeon's can.

'The brain's quite large, you know. The stomach's enormous. People don't realise.'

His wife is plump and chirpy. They've planned this journey for ages, she reveals. The Haseldenes told them about Istanbul.

'It's the last time out for the Orient Express,' the anaesthetist tells me.

'I didn't know that.'

'Well, the last but one or two. Something of that order.'

'You're into millimetres when it comes to eyes,' the colonic surgeon avers. 'There's no margin of error for an eye man.'

His practice is in Birmingham, but the launderette seems to be in Bournemouth. I form the impression that it's an inherited launderette, but don't like to verify this in case queries are considered nosey. Last night I ate my sandwiches on my own, listening to their exchanges through the closed communicating doors; I feel I'm on sufferance now.

'We go somewhere every year,' the surgeon's wife remarks. 'People recommend somewhere, and the three of us set off.'

Last year it was Ghent, the year before the Canary Islands. They'll spend three days in Istanbul and that'll be that; they never stay long; a change is all that's necessary, and the Haseldenes said the Orient Express was coming to an end and should be experienced before it went, Istanbul as well of course. In the past, the Haseldenes said, there was a dining-car and all the trimmings on the Orient Express. Bit of an adventure now.

'We'll need more wine.' The surgeon drains a bottle, and hopes wine can be bought en route.

'You're not to go wandering about the platforms.' Suddenly stern, his wife lays down the law. 'Remember Innsbruck, for heaven's sake!'

'The Bulgarian stuff's meant to be good,' the anaesthetist throws in, glancing at her amusedly, and sounding naughty.

'You will neither of you stir from this train in Bulgaria! Absolutely not!'

'Bull's blood they call it.'

But the surgeon says he thinks Bull's blood comes from Romania, and the protests of his wife and the argument about the origins of Bull's blood continue until it's time to draw across the communicating doors.

The sleeping-car attendant of Voiture 89 quietly wishes us good-night, the corridor is silent. The anaesthetist drops off over the *Journal of the Country Gentleman's Association*. Three nights' jogging on a train couldn't fail to be beneficial to the liver, the surgeon has assured me, and with that in mind, I drop off myself.

In the morning the lavatory at the end of Voiture 89 is blocked. It is not entirely out of action, but when the flush is operated the water rises perilously. The sleeping-car attendant isn't confident about a repair.

The anaesthetist and I leave our compartment unattended while we search for other facilities, and when we return it is occupied by two foreign girls. The anaesthetist is outraged. He takes against the girls even more than he has taken against the American women next door. Unless the girls are ousted immediately they will claim the compartment as theirs; he has seen it happen before, many times in fact. He harangues the girls, and I draw his attention to the fact that they don't understand English, or even French, and in any case have gone to sleep.

'You go,' the anaesthetist shouts at them. 'You go. Shoo! Shoo!'

The girls reply in sign language, heads on one side, making slim little pillows of their hands. Just a little, they plead with their eyes, just a little rest.

'This compartment paid for,' the anaesthetist retaliates. 'Paris to Istanbul, every mile. You clear along now.'

The girls, who are dark-haired and very pretty, sit upright, close together, their closeness suggesting that there is room for four. They show us their tickets: they are travelling only as far as Venice. It seems a useful compromise, but the anaesthetist will have none of it. Muttering crossly, their prettiness lost in a scowl, the girls leave.

Later that day wine is taken on at Sofia, the surgeon's wife jittery and cross while the two men naughtily roam the platforms. In the evening we dine together again, my sandwiches a little sodden, the Fortnum and Mason lettuce lank. In the corridor the American women are entertaining two Turks.

'Repellent sight,' the anaesthetist reports, having been to look. 'The little one's on heat.'

A soft cooing comes from the corridor when we listen, and continues when we close the connecting doors and prepare for the night. On my way down the train I have to squeeze past the bigger of the two American women, whose new friendship has not advanced as rapidly as her companion's. She has other things on her mind.

'You're passing by the fullest holding tank east of Kansas,' she booms at me, and I tell her there are other lavatories on the train. But she says not for her there aren't.

Halfway through the next morning the coffee-car is there. The tiny cups of thick brew are stimulating but not refreshing. Nevertheless the colonic surgeon and his wife, the anaesthetist and I, the American women and their Turks, the suede-clad Italians, the Frenchman with the ciné-camera and all the other travellers from Voiture 89, drink cup after cup of it while we pass through deserty scrubland. Occasionally there's a goat, and once a band of ambling horsemen. 'Bandits' the anaesthetist insists. The Frenchman's camera whirrs.

In the early afternoon we reach Istanbul, and disperse. I ask the way to the Pera Palas, which was once one of the great hotels of Europe and is said to retain a certain majesty, even though a down-at-heel quality predominates. This is true.

The splendour of a vast marble staircase encircles a grandiose liftshaft, the lift itself occasionally not working. Music plays: strict-rhythm dance tunes of the Thirties and Forties, Henry Hall, Victor Silvester. Stuck with Scotch tape to the fading gold of a pillar, a note says: *Wing's Tours. All meet here for dinner, eight sharp, Gillian.* There's a bell you can push if you require the stables.

In the evening the vast, square bar is empty, its sumptuousness dimmed a little by the prominence of a huge refrigerator. Kings once stayed at the Pera Palas, the barman tells me. 'Few kings are left,' he sadly adds. It's the snazzy new Hilton that attracts the out-of-season Pipeline conference, men gathered from four continents to talk about piping oil.

Outside, in Taksim and Beyoglu, rusting taxi-cabs tear wildly through the night streets, and the air is thick with the scent of roasting corn. Promenading men play with short strings of beads or pause to have their shoes brightened. 'I tell you what I do with you,' a beautiful youth remarks, and I explain that I don't want anything done with me.

The wives of the Pipeline men throng the bazaars. Down by the Bosphorus I listen while a French girl, hippily frayed, tells me she has no money. Her eyes are glazed, stale marijuana drifts from her hair. She calls me her friend, she takes my hand. I give her a little.

'How do you do, sir?' a man enquires, and introduces himself as Mr Contractor of Bombay. I have a drink with Mr Contractor and then we eat fish together. Mr Contractor is in Turkey on business. He explains that his business is smuggling and he's anxious to know if my business is smuggling too. He places some cotton-wool on the table between us and takes from it a small piece of glass with an air-bubble in it.

'Hundred twenty dollars, sir. Guaranteed diamond, sir.' I make up for the disappointment that my lack of enthusiasm has caused by telling him about the men of the Pipeline conference. I assure Mr Contractor that a hundred and twenty dollars for a diamond with an air-bubble in it might well seem a bargain to one of them.

Four or so hours away by jet and not at all like Istanbul, Tehran is clean and orderly and new. A laughing porter leads me to my hotel room. 'Iran is good?' he enquires, and I reply that it probably is. I am just beginning to unpack when a woman with a glass of what looks like gin and tonic in one hand, and nothing at all on her body, steps out of the bathroom, humming. I apologise greatly: it's the kind of thing that probably does tend to happen in modern Persia, I try to say, with hotel staff new to the business. She says she intends to have me arrested.

Tehran is proud of itself. Its taxis aren't falling to pieces like the taxis of Istanbul, grass is coaxed to the surface in its arid parks. 'Discipline must be inbred in all,' the Sovereign lays down, and his lovely bride attempts to do something to ease the lot of Iranian women, for Tehran is a man's city in what is still a man's country. Men swagger gracefully, elegantly dressed. Two policemen with wreaths of flowers around their necks stroll about the Takht-E-Jamshid, holding hands.

I listen to an Iranian girl telling me about the efforts of Iranian Woman's Lib. I'm on her side, but she's amazed when I ask her if there's been any bra-burning. 'But they'd look terrible without them,' she says, giggling at a bunch of schoolgirls in Western school uniform. The girls are beautiful, young women already, shy-eyed but without the awkwardness of adolescence. As we watch, two boys jostle arrogantly through them. In one generation, the girl tells me, it'll be different: to start with, all Iranian women will be liberated from the shackles, not of the bra, but of the veil. I find it difficult to believe.

It's more difficult still as you move over desert-brown, ugly landscape, down south to Isfahan, that small old town with more atmosphere than anywhere else I know, where the opium poppies grow. Walk away from the centre, from the great Shah Abbas Hotel, from the tourist miniatures and the Persian rugs with the faces of Kennedy and Eisenhower on them, walk less than half a mile and you're suddenly in the midst of a conglomeration of life where everything is happening at once.

While you wait a man will make you a pair of shoes, and the man who shaves you under a tree doesn't know what lather is. Another man kills a hen for you, although a dead hen isn't really what you want. The hurrying women, squeezing pieces of liver and other intestines before agreeing to purchase them, have a tight-lipped look because of their tightly-gathered veils. One lowers hers and smiles, but this isn't the liberation that the girl in Tehran was so concerned about.

The Americans and the Germans and the French suck Isfahan dry. Their moving cameras whirr in the Friday Mosque and the Shah Mosque and the Sheikh Lotfollah. 'Hullo, hullo,' children cry at them. 'Iran good, misters?' Everyone agrees that Iran is good, but one tetchy Frenchman, brought to see a typical Persian house because the Chehel Sotoun is closed, complains that the house is just an ordinary house. Sensibly, the guide pretends not to understand.

If you leave Isfahan on the five o'clock bus in the morning you'll be in Shiraz in time for lunch. Shiraz is where the nightingales are, and the roses and the wine and the poetry. As well, for me, there's Hermann, the tallest dentist in Austria. I'm with him when he picks up his mail at Shiraz post office. We drink sherbet while he reads these letters, all of which he has written himself. It's a habit with him, he explains, like the habit other people have of talking to themselves. One day he hopes to marry a pretty girl and the habit won't be necessary any more.

Cats crawl about us while we sip our sherbet and a holy man reads powerfully from the Koran. Hermann engages the woman at the next table in conversation. She is small and attractive. Her husband is a kind man, she tells Hermann and me, in the bathroom-fittings business in Tehran. But he's much older than she is and she's only really happy when she can think of him as a father. Unable to resist a dream of Persian luxury, she married for money. Now she has run away, but unfortunately the young engineer she was to meet in romantic Shiraz hasn't turned up.

All three of us search this rose-clad town for an engineer, and he proves so patently absent that I begin to wonder if he isn't just the heart of a Persian housewife's fantasy. But as she catches the early-morning plane back to Tehran I know he's real enough: his treachery is deep in her eyes, side by side with the mistake she made when she settled for luxury. 'So beautiful,' Hermann wistfully murmurs. 'So beautiful when they're sad.'

They've built an Intercontinental hotel within striking distance of Persepolis, but you still don't have to walk there: you hire a car, and the car waits for you while you saunter through what remains of the city of Parsa. *Travellers who came to Iran in the time of Alexander the Macedonian called it Persepolis*, my guidebook reminds me, *which is the expression used by all foreigners who come to visit this site.*

A battalion of the Shah's army is there now, roaming about the ruins in well-pressed uniforms, obligingly posing for photographs whenever they are asked to. *After founding a wide empire extending from the Sind Valley to beyond the Nile, and from the Oxus to the banks of the Danube, the Archaemenians — a notable and distinguished tribal division of the Persian people — determined to build in their birthplace a monument to themselves surpassing all the capitals of the countries of the ancient East.*

Translated by the Reverend R. Sharp, M.A., Cantab., the guidebook isn't an easy read. *Accordingly on a site beside the Mountain of Mercy (Kuh-i-Rahmat), overlooking the wide green plain of Marvdasht, which for thousands of years prior to the Archaemenians had been the cradle of a conspicuous culture and art, the plan of a great palace was drawn up, and the first stone of the largest hall there was laid by the powerful hand of Darius the Great between the years 514 and 512 BC . . . Some examples of the past civilisation and the crafts, both before and after the building of Persepolis, exist in other parts of the world, but practically no monument can be seen which approaches the grandeur and importance of Persepolis. This is a collection of evidences of the art and culture and standard of skill and proficiency of the craftsmen and of the ambition of the kings.*

Persepolis is enormous and once was even larger. In the Hall of a Hundred Columns a mythical beast engages the attention of an unflinching guard. In the palace of the Apadana a regiment of Susian soldiers marches stonily on and on, while helmeted Scythians stand ready by their horses. The bricks of the Queen's Apartments are sun-dried, and in the Central Palace nobles and high Median officers decorate a staircase. Bulls and lions are in conflict; Darius is enthroned, with his sceptre and his lotus leaf. On friezes everywhere figures bear gifts and valuables, above cuneiform inscriptions in Old Persian or Babylonian. 'The Tachara is the Winter Palace,' a guide informs his followers. 'Here the stone was so deeply polished that for centuries after a person might look for his reflection in it. So it came to be named the Hall of Mirrors.

But that, we must know, is not an ancient name. It is a name of our present times.'

Beyond the shade of these palatial ruins the midday sun is searingly hot. Unaffected, the men of the Shah's army relax in it, practising their pidgin English on the visitors. The waiting cars have been driven beneath tarpaulins.

'Impossible to imagine,' my driver quietly comments. 'No one can imagine Persepolis.'

When I try to, Hollywood crowd scenes fill the great vacuum that has been left, and the real people of Persepolis refuse to emerge — its high officers, its hidden women, its emperors, its craftsmen, its storytellers, its prophets, the interpreters of its dreams, the accountants of its Treasury, the merchants of its bazaars, the criminals of its cells, its servants and its slaves. All craftsmen and artisans received adequate daily wages, the Reverend Sharp assures us, whether they worked with gold or stone, carved cedar beams or made carpets, hung tapestries or laid floors. Persepolis basked for a hundred and eighty years in its glory, until Alexander burnt the whole place down in 331 BC.

Back in Shiraz, tall Hermann has found a companion. It is the smaller of the two Americans of Voiture 89, and her companion does not seem pleased. She's in the hotel business, she grumpily tells me over tea, and when I respond by recounting my hotel experience in Tehran she assures me that the double booking of a hotel room couldn't occur in Pennsylvania or anywhere else in the United States. 'That poor *woman!*' she cries, glaring at me.

Moving west, I wonder about the lady whose lover was not in Shiraz and about the anaesthetist who reads toothpaste tubes, and his companions. Flames dance about the sky, above the high chimneys of the Gulf's refineries. 'No women in Bushehr,' a local oilman informs me. He travels with vodka and hashish in a basket, intent on a few days among the fleshpots of Abadan. In darkened bars sit other oilmen and tired French tarts in feather dresses. Pop groups from Tehran play Greek music. The men play cards.

The next day the desert-brown landscape recedes and with it the dreaminess of ancient Persia, the brilliant blue domes, the slender minarets, the tomb of Darius, the Apadana Palace. Brisk, modern Iran recedes also, the well-kept taxis, IranAir's punctual aeroplanes. In Athens it's raining, and it's still raining in Rome.

(1970)

New York, 1973

IN THE EARLY morning the drama of New York has run down. Manhattan is without its gloss, the mellow air of an Indian summer has an unused smell.

Downtown in Delancey Street little Miss Shulz, a teller in the Chemical Bank, sleeps chastely on. In Greenwich Village Miss Ariadne Graff-Bosco, born Suzie Meyer, dreams of an Indian jazz singer. On the steps of the City Library the New York pigeons are the same as pigeons everywhere.

It is a hard city in the early morning. Puerto Ricans roll off the night shifts, others clock in. Over on the West Side sheets of dull brown pasteboard are loaded on to lorries. At all-night dogstands eaters eat in silence, dwarfed by skyscrapers that keep the sunshine off the streets. No one smiles because there's nothing to smile at.

Two hundred years ago the city wasn't there, and the Empire State Building wasn't there before 1931. It's a date of a little significance because the Thirties meant a lot to this city: the cocktail had come to stay, with the skyscraper, and Fred Astaire and Ginger Rogers. Show business and the Thirties went into New York's bloodstream, cheering away the great Wall Street disaster, and cheering even now — while Harlem seethes and the refuse problem gets worse with every hour.

In Central Park this autumn morning boys play football on bald clay, organised by three middle-aged men. One man is big, another has short grey hair, the third is nondescript. The men shout nasally, pitching the ball about, whipping up enthusiasm. The boys chew. Any moment now, an elderly onlooker remarks, the big man will drop dead, the way he's taxing his pump. 'You wait. You'll see,' this old man warns, settling himself for the tragedy. The men are weight-losing executives, doing their morning bit to keep down crime: the boys are delinquents in need of human warmth.

'You hear the newest?' the old man asks, and repeats the abuse a late-night journalist has showered on the President. The President's Watergate is the greatest talking point in the whole history of the American nation. 'This fellow was sayin',' the old man continues, 'what I hadn't noticed before: sweat comes out on the upper lip when he's tense. You ever notice that, Presidential lip-sweat?'

★

The abusing of the President is almost a game: Go back three spaces, Stop robbing the bank. The President seems bankrupt already, the game's the nation's. *Impeachment with Honor* the plastic buttons say, ten cents from the street-traders on Seventh Avenue. Mao Tse-Tung is pushing drugs, the John Birch Society claims, a death trade that has been encouraged by the Nixon Administration because the Nixon Administration favours commerce with Red China.

On West 34th Street you can learn how to get a New York divorce for a hundred dollars, but nobody cares much. Paper-backed and urgent, *Vaginal Politics* is equally ignored. The people of West 34th Street are talking about the late-night journalist and the sweat that comes when the President is tense. 'Imagine it,' one citizen unsmilingly remarks, 're-designing the Presidential plane at a time like this.' Short-haired, in shirtsleeves, clean young executives agree in their washrooms that no corporation president would get away with it.

Fifth Avenue gleams in mid-morning sunshine, Madison is busier. In Lord and Taylor's, New Jersey wives sip fruit juices and leave the President alone. They talk in the Bird Cage and the Soup Bowl, of girdles and corselets and brassieres, and shoes and percale sheets, and Christmas gifts, and food and dieting. Once they were like Miss Shulz of Delancey Street and the Chemical Bank: petite and pretty, the girls who swooned for Frank Sinatra. 'He has *so*. He's gone,' one whispers to a friend. 'Poor Agnes!'

Agnes should be sitting there herself, in powder blue, forty-four and a bit, a hundred and sixty pounds: she'd be there if he hadn't gone off with a petite and pretty Miss Shulz, or a Miss Foster or a Miss Claiborne. Over the non-fattening fruit juices the feeling is that Agnes — who won a prize in 1949 for her resemblance to Elizabeth Taylor — will never again hold her head up in the Bird Cage or the Soup Bowl, or at least not until he returns.

'You're welcome,' Miss Shulz says brightly two blocks away, behind her teller's counter. She says it all day, and smiles as the Chemical Bank has taught her to smile. She dreams of being rescued from the bank and Delancey Street by Mr Right in a Volkswagen. But sometimes, just now and then, Miss Shulz's dream goes chilly on her. She has heard too often of women like Agnes, and the New York divorce you can get for a hundred dollars. Marriage, sex pundits such as Ariadne Graff-Bosco say, is a non-event.

Fifth Avenue and Madison are full of Miss Shulzes and Miss Fosters and Miss Claibornes. They're smart and they're smartly dressed, and they'll tell you New York's the most exciting city in the world, adding that it's a fun city and a city of Now. The tourist promoters agree. The violence is exaggerated, they softly insist: come backstage on Broadway and we'll show you the exact spot where Debbie Reynolds danced last night.

Scum, all scum; and the violence is meaningful, says Ariadne Graff-Bosco — which is something she can prove. Ariadne Graff-Bosco has a thin pale face and black hair that grows horizontally from the two sides of her head. She is thirty-two and at present not employed. Her mother has just gone missing in Philadelphia, her child — now ten — is in custody somewhere. She is blackly dressed as she yawns in front of her television set — in mourning, so she claims, for the quality of her life. A man she met has tickets for some unspeakable theatre and wants to buy her cocktails before the show. He's from out-of-town somewhere, she can't remember where. Brown-flannelled of course, for the world is full of brown-flannelled men, which is the trouble, God knows, with the world.

In the Rainbow Room at the top of the Rockefeller Center there's a cocktail-hour convention of bank employees. Miss Shulz is dazzling in red, smiling her smile and sipping a whiskey sour. The bank employees abuse the President, but Miss Shulz does not. Miss Shulz is unique: Miss Shulz feels sorry for the President, but in the Rainbow Room she does not say so. Music plays at the bank employees' convention. In Harlem a man is murdered.

The man who has tickets for a theatre arrives in Greenwich Village to pick up Ariadne. He's fifteen years older than Ariadne and comes, as he now reminds her, from Nashville. He's in the ballpoint business, a freckled man whose name Ariadne is determined never to know. To his surprise she doesn't turn off the television when they leave her room. Such stuff is the *scum* of empty rooms, Ariadne whispers huskily in the taxi, huskily adding that that, if ever there was one, is a redeemable phrase.

The cocktail hour goes on and on. In bars and hotels and apartments, Sidecars and White Ladies are seriously consumed, and highballs and lowballs. 'Jack Daniel's on the rocks,' the escort of Ariadne orders, and Ariadne herself calls for a treble gin and tonic. In the Christmassy atmosphere of the Rainbow Room a bank employee, high up in the Chase Manhattan, finds Miss Shulz another whiskey sour and invites her to have dinner with him.

★

Everything is suddenly happening at once. In her sweet little Alice-blue gown Debbie Reynolds sings. Michele Lee and Tommy Tune sing, even Glynis Johns sings. Hundreds of voices are all of a sudden singing on Broadway. Z Z Top is experiencing his finest hour in the form of a one-night stand. Bisexual liberation is to be had for free in the Consciousness-Raising Workshops, and in a church Lib-men and Lib-women share thoughts and feelings for three dollars at the door. There are talks on herbal medicine, and on Marxism, Leninism and Revisionism. Israel Jacobs demonstrates psychic healing in Broome Street. 'Adam's Rib' is brought to the emptiness of Ariadne's room by the headache tablet Bufferin, but the man called Jacob Fuchsberg — who keeps interrupting — has nothing to do with 'Adam's Rib' or the headache tablet Bufferin. Jacob Fuchsberg is a real man. He has taken advertising space to ask the emptiness to make him the state's Chief Judge.

New York is her own fiery cocktail now. In her taxis iron curtains fall into place, protecting the driver from his fares. In Times Square, massive TV police-vans trundle into position, their cameras cocked to locate crime. Tired ladies in tights and G-strings dance like lifesize dolls on the counter of a bar, hugely reflected in the mirrors behind them. Tired men stare at the G-strings and sometimes hand up a dollar-bill to receive, in return, a personalised smile.

In pornographic cinemas other men sit in cathedral earnestness, alone with *The Devil in Miss Jones*. Unlike the G-string men, they seek some grail from this devil's wonders: new life or understanding, new hope, or God. On the Broadway sidewalks the first trickle of the city's night-walkers arrives, seeking something also. Far down on the Bowery an old alcoholic seeks oblivion in a doorway, crouched in the darkness, trusting he won't have the nuisance of waking up again. In East 14th Street a mugger mugs.

Miss Shulz does not have dinner in Sardi's, but Ariadne Graff-Bosco does. 'I don't know where I heard it,' Ariadne is saying. 'You part in order to meet again. That, too, is a redeemable phrase.' Her escort silently smiles. He doesn't get all this stuff about redeemable phrases. He wants to talk about himself and he does, telling Ariadne about a loveless marriage and teenage drop-out children in Nashville. Ariadne doesn't listen. She thinks of flying to Philadelphia to find her mother. In her white face her eyes are black, like her hair. She composed a dance which was performed, she says. 'Redeemable Phrases' she called it.

Sardi's, with caricatures of everyone who ever was or is, reflects the Broadway razzmatazz. Applause breaks out as first-night leading ladies enter. 'That's Henry Fonda,' a short-sighted woman insists. 'Hey, is that guy Henry Fonda?' she demands of a waiter, and the waiter obligingly says sure, it's Mr Fonda. But the woman's husband points out that Henry Fonda is a thin man and this is a fat man. 'You're thinking of Pat O'Brien, for Christ's sake!' Pat O'Brien is no longer alive, but the waiter says sure, the guy's Mr O'Brien.

Bit-part actresses smile menacingly in Sardi's, their very black or very blonde hair gleaming as though polished. Their lips look polished too, and their cheeks and their foreheads. It's difficult being beautiful in Sardi's when nobody knows who you are. 'Scum, all scum,' comments Ariadne Graff-Bosco.

In Times Square the eyes of the television cameras peer into the gathering crowds of night-walkers. In Times Square and all around it the young black night-boys are strangely dressed, some in costume with an eighteenth-century flavour, others in frills and jackboots. Girls and women, all shades and ages, loiter in groups, a few attired as cowhands, others in beads. Hats are popular, and musk is in the air.

Neon gleams whitely on endless cinema fronts, brighter than the daytime sun. Other neon is garish, red and yellow, green and blue and purple, promoting chewing-gum and beer. Smoke belches from the mouth of a neon cigarette-smoker, half a building high. The news is there in neon too, for anyone who wants it.

No one does. It isn't unrest in the Middle East that interests the night-walkers, but the sale or acquisition of drugs and sex, or just the fun of exhibiting themselves. With their brass-topped canes and buckled shoes, they live their fantasies, a nightly respite from days in a pasteboard factory or a kitchenware department. Among junkies and knife-carriers and prostitutes, the ordinary play at being extraordinary. Each night claims its handful of victims, and the next night a few more of the ordinary are there for real.

'I'd rather not.' Miss Shulz is firm in Delancey Street, and the man who's high up in the Chase Manhattan, who has spent twenty dollars on her in the Cattleman West, is unable not to be cross. She's keeping all that for her wedding night, Miss Shulz explains. She smiles. He swears as he clatters down the iron stairway.

In P J Clarke's all-night saloon Ariadne drinks Old Number 7 and says that after another glass or two she'd take it kindly if her escort would permit her to return with him to his hotel room, to make a telephone call. P J Clarke's is full of the razzmatazz people — blues singers and piano-players, nightclub performers and a few of the bit-part actresses who earlier smiled menacingly in Sardi's. For the fifth time Ariadne's escort says he does not love his wife, nor does his wife love him; and, what is not often known, the ballpoint industry in Nashville isn't as healthy as it might be. Old Number 7 stains the brown flannel of his suit. It is 4.00 a.m. in P J Clarke's and nobody is tired.

★

Sirens scream as trouble breaks in Times Square. A lung is pierced, four fighters are arrested. A girl, staggering on her own, falls with a thump to the pavement. A man with ravenous eyes agrees at last on a price: a hundred dollars for two hours of flagellation. The night-walkers drift away.

From her escort's hotel room Ariadne telephones England: the Metropolitan Hotel, Brighton. The Indian jazz singer she loves is there, or so he has said. But the Metropolitan Hotel, Brighton, knows nothing about an Indian jazz singer. 'You part in order to meet again,' Ariadne whispers huskily in her escort's hotel room, weeping whiskey tears. She feels as though she has dreamed the Indian jazz singer.

Dreams are exploding everywhere in the world's most exciting city. You dream of love and end with stained brown flannel. You dream of

Mr Right, but the long-hallowed theory of Mr Right has been exploded. Dreamtime was the Thirties. There's the reality of the waste-disposal unit now, and the washing-machine, two cars for every family, the hundred dollar divorce. It's a reality seen every day, in everyone's home — the better world of the television ads. You, too, though you live in Harlem, have a right to it. You, too, whoever you are, have a right to say that your President's sweat is the sweat of guilt. From the steamy presses of the pasteboard factory you parade Broadway like the prince you might once have only dared to imagine you were. In the world's most exciting city dreams become rights with a bang.

(1973)

In Search of Siri

O N THE WAY from Arlanda Airport to the SAS Terminal the man beside me said he was a Finnish sea captain. He'd been in Bangkok, he said, where the weather was sultry. In Stockholm in February it was naturally cold: he advised the purchase of a fur hat. He took from a carrier-bag a bottle of Johnny Walker Black Label whisky. 'Do you mind much,' he politely enquired, 'if I give myself a little drink, sir?' I shook my head. He drank and handed the bottle to me, and then the bottle passed to a man sitting across the aisle from us and to a woman with a child behind us. 'I am here for good time,' the Finnish sea captain said, drinking some more before setting the bottle on its round again. 'Then two months by wife in countryside.'

We passed forests laden with snow and wide fields on which the drifts lay high and smooth, elegantly shaped by the wind. It was dusk, snow was lightly falling, the bus was pleasantly warm. Again offering his whisky, the sea captain asked me if I was English and when I explained I was Irish he became excited because in Bangkok he'd been reading in a newspaper about Ireland. 'There's fighting there,' he said. 'Catholics and Protestants. Are you here for that, sir? To make a case? Why you in Stockholm, sir?'

I said I'd come in pursuit of an actress called Siri von Essen. 'Finnish,' I said. 'Like you.'

'You love this actress, sir?'

'She's dead.'

'The funeral —'

'No, no. She died a long time ago. She was the wife of Sweden's great playwright, August Strindberg. A strange marriage.'

'All marriages are strange, sir.'

'Yes.'

The SAS Terminal is so far outside Stockholm that no matter

which part of the city you're going to it's necessary to take a taxi. 'I am going to the Grand Hotel,' a tall man in the queue called out, seeking a companion with whom to share the fare. 'Anyone here for the Grand Hotel?' The air was like a razor on the flesh; we shuffled our feet on the hard-packed snow, keeping the circulation going. The Finnish sea captain said good-bye. In Stockholm, he assured me, a good time was easy to find. My turn for a taxi came.

I was writing for BBC Television a play about Strindberg's first marriage, to Siri von Essen. I wanted to see for myself the parks they'd walked in, the Royal Theatre where she'd acted in a few of his plays, the house of her aristocratic first husband the Baron Wrangel, the rooms of the National Museum, in which, with their backs to Madonnas, I had imagined them speaking of love. In some way, I hoped, being in Stockholm might bring me even an inch nearer to the mystery of their relationship. Why had Strindberg, placing so much store by the notion of marriage with a good woman, so perversely chosen a bad one? And was she really as bad as he'd claimed?

In the huge tiled T-Centralen, the central underground station, a prostitute was dancing. She wasn't sober; pairs of policemen, revolvers in shiny white holsters, eyed her bleakly. Youths sang and swayed together in gangs, arms interlocked, their faces flushed. The prostitute fell, two policemen arrested her. Strindberg had wondered if Siri had once been a whore: had her mother, left badly off in a Finnish town, put her on to the streets for a month or so at a hard-pressed time? The notion, like hundreds of others concerning her, became an obsession with him.

Young men and girls sat in parked cars, drinking light beer from cans. For fun they'd drive recklessly around the clock, car chasing car, brakes screeching, the tyres skidding on ice. They watched for police cars and drove carefully away when one moved into sight. It was a Sunday night, a time for games and relaxation. People hurried to a concert of Mozart and Haydn, others strolled aimlessly, not minding the cold, pausing by well-lit shop windows to examine furniture and television sets.

Beneath the glass and steel skyscrapers of Hötorget, the centre of modern Stockholm, a young man wept while a girl caressed him: a love affair was at an end. He walked away, down wide concrete steps, motioning at her not to follow him. Snow collected on the girl's fur hood as she watched her lover go, fading into the crowd like a hero in a film. Siri and Strindberg had parted too, often and bitterly.

He had called her his Satan blonde, this curly-haired girl from Finland who'd managed to marry into the Swedish upper classes and was bored when she found herself there. She was fascinated by the theatre, stage-struck but frustrated, because as the wife of an army officer a career for her as an actress was out of the question. Strindberg, an official in the Royal Library and a struggling writer, cut a romantic figure in her eyes, especially when viewed beside the stout, red-cheeked Baron Wrangel. He thought of her as a child when first he saw her, even though she had herself already given birth to a child: he saw her as the virginal mother, the gentle wife, respectful yet intelligent, a beautiful Madonna. In his autobiographical novel *The Confession of a Fool* he describes a meeting in the National Museum:

> I adored her as I saw her coming up the marble staircase, under the gilded ceiling, as I watched her little feet tripping over the flags of variegated stucco, her fine figure clothed in a black velvet costume trimmed with military braid. I hurried to meet her and, like a page, bent my knees before her. Her beauty, which had blossomed under my kisses, was striking. The rich blood in her veins shone through transparent cheeks. This statue of a young old maid had quickened under my caresses and grown warm at the fire of life. Pygmalion had breathed on the marble and held a goddess in his arms.

I saw, the next day, the Madonnas of the National Museum: the Virgin Odigitria, the Virgin by Giacomo da Ponte, the Virgin by the Master of the Legend of St Catherine. I walked by the frozen sea on which huge rocks of ice were scattered, where boats lay clogged till summer. The sun shone from a clear sky; children threw bread to flocks of birds. Spring would arrive in a couple of months: there was a hint of it already, people said. In spring in Stockholm, women see themselves in a new light: their winter clothes seem shabby in the balmy freshness, they feel they've been in hiding. A girl leaned against the timbered side of a hut, her eyes closed, her face lifted towards the pale blue sky. She smoked, basking in the moment of warmth, pretending spring had come already.

From high gutters on the roofs of houses men shovelled snow, or worked with pick-axes to loosen slabs of ice. On the street youths roared out a warning to the passers-by, gesturing them off the pavements as the ice came down. I stopped to watch. From below you couldn't see the wires that kept the workmen safe, attached to their waists and to a chimney-stack. They worked intently, not pausing to talk.

I turned away from the dockside, walking inland, skirting the Nobel-parken. In the Television Centre I was to see a new documentary about Strindberg and Siri, based on their letters. 'How do you like Stockholm?' a pretty girl asked me, and I said it was beautiful. 'You should have come in spring,' she said.

The girl translated while we watched. Reeds swayed gently in a wind, lake water gently lapped: the film, in the classic Swedish style, was poignant and reverent. 'They hate each other now,' the girl said in a slightly American accent. 'He is mad, she says. He accuses her of lesbianism.' I listened while a Swedish voice continued and the girl translated: the virginal mother had become the Satan blonde, the Madonna was a skin stretched over evil.

He had encouraged her to seek her freedom as a woman, he'd helped her to become an actress, a 'new woman' in the Ibsen fashion. But his Pygmalion creation rounded on him; his goddess had talons. For the rest of his life he ranted against Ibsen — 'the Norwegian blue-stocking' — as an absurd and dangerous influence and a destroyer of marriage. But the villain of the piece wasn't Ibsen, nor indeed was it Strindberg or Siri. They loved one another, they married, without ever knowing that they were enemies, not friends. The villain of the piece was sex itself, some aspect of it that turned sour and ugly, until there was perversion within perversion, and madness played a part.

Watching the film I remembered that, before his marriage, the hero of *The Confession of a Fool* had attempted suicide. Presented to us as a man of honour, the sin of being in love with a married woman was too much for him: naked, he swam at night in a rough sea and then sat among the rocks in the rain, praying for pneumonia so that he might later slowly die, while her hands cooled his forehead.

*

That day Swedish workmen were pulling down his house in the Karlaplan. I watched them, thinking still of the strange attempt at suicide. I saw him in a tempestuous sea; from Bach's Magnificat a choir sang 'Omnes Generationes', becoming louder and louder as he swam to rescue himself from too quick a death. What visions did he see as the wild rain fell upon him? Siri as he would have had her, a serene Madonna by Baldovinetti? Siri with an infant child begat by him, happy in his love for her?

Afterwards he lay in a bed in a nearby inn. A clergyman prayed with him, and from the holy words he took some comfort even though at that time in his life he did not believe in God. This was another complication in the rack of his life: he was a man who needed religion as others need water, yet he could not easily have faith. The clergyman was a simple pastor of the countryside, who could make little of this intense young man who had swum in the sea at night and then had sat naked among rocks. 'What is your sin?' he asked, but the man in the bed replied only that soon a woman would come to the inn with her husband, the Baron Wrangel: they must be shown to his room, he ordered, even if he slept.

The workmen's sledge-hammers rose and fell, the house was almost gone. Yellow lorries carried it away, bricks and rubble, old panelling and doors. 'A shame,' the pretty girl at the Television Centre had said. 'A shame to do a thing like that.' It was the same, I suggested to her, the world over.

Stockholm is ornate, rococo, then suddenly severe and modern. Everything is expensive and as though in reflection of that, people seem a trifle dour. Alcohol plays a part in the lives of many; there are long parties, with drink and sauna and sexual variations; there is often an air of boredom. All this was part of the marriage of Siri and Strindberg. There was, on the one hand, the idyll of their love, like spring, and on the other the dark depressions of winter and the effort to escape them. Siri had another child, but she was boarded out by day because Siri, who had already made her theatrical debut, wished to continue her career on the stage. Strindberg tutored her, endeavouring in particular to rid her of her Finnish accent.

I walked through the Royal Theatre, and sat in the Berns Salonger, the great gilt-covered restaurant in Berzeliipark where Strindberg regularly attended. In the Gamla Stan, the old town, narrow streets wound steeply and alleys were picturesque. Soldiers guarded the baroque splendour of the Royal Palace, stamping through the floodlit night. Flares burned on the balconies of smart hotels. Snow, sea, architecture — dignity was everywhere. And then, in hard contrast, there was the sleazy pornography in the windows of newspaper booths and tobacconists'. *Sex around the Clock Tonight! Lesson 14: Sexual Positions for February, 1970! Big News from Spanking City!* Magazine covers in orgasmic full cry and garish colour were urgently displayed for all, children too, to see. The hint of decadence about it all brought me back to Siri von Essen. Had she been a woman whose cruelty drove her husband mad? Had she taken a sexual delight in that, or had Strindberg crazily exaggerated?

I tried to imagine their life together after their first child, Karin, was born. His novel, *The Red Room*, had been published and acclaimed. He was no longer poor. He had written *The Secret of the Guild* with Siri in mind and had submitted it to the Royal Theatre; he was proud that an article of his had been read before the Académie des Inscriptions et Belles-Lettres of the Institut de France.

> Having at the age of thirty won an excellent position in the literary and scientific world and with a brilliant future before me, I found the greatest happiness in laying my trophies at (Siri's) feet . . . But she was angry with me because I had upset the equilibrium of our marriage. I had to make myself smaller and smaller to spare her the humiliation of belonging to a man who was superior to her . . . She liked to belittle me in front of the servants and visiting friends, especially her woman friends.

The idyll of their love was falling apart, coming together, falling apart again. 'I deliberately fostered in her the delusion that I had her to thank for my fame, which she did not understand and which she apparently disparaged. I took positive delight in making myself out to be her inferior. I was happy to be no more than the husband of a charming woman, and eventually she came to believe that she possessed my genius.'

She flirted, deliberately, in his presence: it seemed part of her sensuality that she should humiliate him so, and at times part of his. She had escaped from the heavy upper-class atmosphere of the Baron's house, where his fellow officers drank with him and played cards, where he himself was permitted to eye whatever young girl happened to be about. Her own eyes then had remained conventionally downcast, watching the stitches of her embroidery. She had escaped from that, and she wanted to go on escaping — from every convention and every accepted formality. As her new husband was obsessed with his jealous thoughts so she was obsessed with the notion of further escape and further independence. They battled through a petty day-to-day life: no longer could he persuade himself that she was the 'mother-woman' he had seen her as, the Madonna of his dreams; and for her, his role as rescuer was now played out. But still, in the mounting violence of their quarrels, in all their storming insults, they continued to love one another.

In my Stockholm hotel I dreamed of them. They sat at dinner in a long drawing-room, served by a maid. 'How delicious!' murmured Siri, sniffing a dish of casserole. The Baron had been to the house again, he accused, and she sweetly apologised, saying she'd meant to tell him: he'd been asleep at the time, she said, in the garden. The Baron had brought a gift, a little spaniel that had been owned by both of them in their days together. Wasn't it sweet of the Baron, she murmured, to bring a gift? He shouted at her. Her doctor had been to the house also, while he slept. Was the house a brothel that two such notorious libertines should visit it so easily and so often?

In my dream she smiled again. She tried to talk of something else. 'Do you undress,' he roared at her, 'in front of that lecherous doctor?' And reasonably she explained that for the purposes of a medical examination it was necessary to undress. She was a whore, he shouted, all Stockholm knew; his children were not his.

She came to life then and when she spoke her voice was quiet, though it increased in volume and ended by silencing him. Her pale blue eyes contained nothing but contempt; her performance was that of an actress, her words those of the theatre. 'Every gesture I make,' she said, 'every smile I offer to another person is charged to my account and held against me. But I will tell you this: I am a living woman and there is strength in me to live my life as I wish to live it. I have blood in my veins and flesh on my bones. I have a mind and a heart. I have borne you two children in the first year of our marriage, I have sacrificed myself to your desires. Now it is my turn: people shall come again to this house. The Baron shall come if so I wish, every day if I invite him. And my doctor shall give me whatever treatment is necessary.

And if I wish for Chinese and Arabs, they shall come too, and African war-dancers, and the people of Russia, and Englishmen and French, and proud Spaniards, Sicilians, men of Morocco, Turks and Greeks, and perfumed girls if so I wish. They shall drink our wine and smoke our cigarettes, and in this house where you would have us live like hermits there shall be talk and laughter as there should be. And I shall walk again before the footlights and I shall bear no more children, no matter how you plead.'

They sat in silence then and when the maid came into the room to clear away the dishes Siri rose and went to her, to hand her their plates. 'How pretty you're looking tonight!' she murmured, and in a long mirror that stretched to the ground from the ceiling Strindberg saw his wife lightly embrace their pretty maid, and was amazed.

*

I walked all over Stockholm, thinking about them. There was a kind of inevitability about Siri's plunge into lesbianism, the final move in the game to become the emancipated woman so honoured by the Norwegian blue-stocking. In Strindberg's view such women would live without men, except when, now and again, they cared to seek the means to reproduce their species. She confessed to him that at the theatre she enjoyed embracing other girls; her friends of the theatre came to stay with her; she hired extra servant girls, and soon the house was a hell of women, drinking and chattering, quarrelling over Strindberg's wife. In public, he wrote, she openly flirted with her female admirers, sitting on their laps at parties, permitting herself to be kissed with passion. At such times her eyes were never far from his face, in search of his reactions. He was mad, she told him, when in misery he rebuked her. He had had hallucinations about Madonnas: now they came in another form; in his lunacy he saw evil everywhere. She had triumphed, he wrote, she had won the game: his humiliation as a man was complete. As a wretched gesture, he sold his wedding ring and spent the money in a brothel.

In the Nobelparken I invented her diary. *Soon he will kill me. I can no longer live with this man. I can no longer act out the rôles he gives me for his tormented delectation. I can no longer tolerate his terrifying presence.*

Another girl was sunning her face in a blink of wintry sunshine, leaning against a wall. A young man ran across the snow to her, laughing and calling her name. I wondered if they knew much about the private life of their great playwright, and his time with Siri von Essen.

(1970)

The Valle Verzasca

IT IS FASHIONABLE to be snooty about Switzerland. In one way or another people like to echo the comparison expressed in the film *The Third Man*: after centuries of internecine upheaval, treachery and violence, the Italians produced Leonardo da Vinci and the glories of the Italian Renaissance; after centuries of peace and brotherly love the Swiss gave the world the cuckoo clock. The sentiment is that of Orson Welles, playing the part of Harry Lime; not of Graham Greene, who wrote the script, who chose both to die and be buried among the cuckoo clocks.

Trapped by its mountains, Switzerland has long ago defeated a hostile geography and turned to its own advantage an unenviable position in an often unstable Europe. Cleverness has done it, and the recognition that a daunting landscape is good to look at, that a sunny meadow high up on an alp has a greater appeal than a field. There is no enigma, no contradiction. Sunshine sparkles on the lakes; and as Nature surely intended, the grim terrain becomes a single vast hotel, with full banking facilities, the easiest country in the world to dawdle in.

The Swiss rely for their existence on their neighbours and their visitors, on the wearers of watches, on chocolate-eaters and currency-traders. Their politeness is real, and a pleasure to encounter; but politeness is clothing, and beneath it the Swiss can be mean, cross, holier-than-thou — just like anyone else. Women are raped in Switzerland; thefts take place; there are murders. A twee paradise is there for those who feel comfortable in it, but that Switzerland is also the hard heart of Europe is its saving grace.

Lugano, capital of the Ticino, is sophisticated in the Swiss way, and in what the Swiss are good at there's a lot of choice. Chocolate comes white or milky or dark, chunky with nuts and raisins, syrupy with fruit-juice, bucked up with alcohol, breakfast-flavoured with corn-flakes or rice crispies. There are watches from all the famous names —

gold, bejewelled, the kind you can swim in, the kind that tell you the time all over the world, or watches just for fun. There are clocks that incorporate men chopping wood and women milking cows. There are pigeons stuffed with fish, and snails with truffles, and perfect escalopes, and appetizing lamb, and little fish from the lakes. Lugano is respectably elegant, with paddle-boats on the lake and a civilised cable-car between the town and the railway station. Until recently it possessed the most impressive of Europe's private art collections. Lugano, like Switzerland itself, attends to your needs: you'll be fairly treated and get what you want if you ask for it. You may even be lucky enough to find yourself offered a Magic Hands bed massage: fifteen minutes which 'leaves you feeling fine, just place a single Swiss franc in the convenient bedside slot'.

Locarno and Ascona are around the corner from each other on Lago Maggiore, more modest than Lugano but no less intent on obliging the visitor. Stout Swiss Germans take the full pension at their comfortable hotels — the Muralto, the Beau Rivage, the Schiff, the International. Their cappuccinos are topped with good Swiss cream; the Coppa Romanoff and the banana split, the Coppa Danemark and The Colonel, are not inferior to those of the canton's capital. In warm October sunshine, when the last of summer lingers, the chestnut confections are at their best.

But the Ticino is more than these goodtime resorts. It is notable because it is where the ebullience of Italy merges with Swiss good sense, where the familiar clash of characteristics to be found among border people has developed an idiosyncrasy of its own. It's the language that does it: the Swiss, speaking Italian, are their own people — Italian yet belonging to their confederacy, leaner than the Northerners they welcome, their features reflecting the dictates of a more musical tongue, their southern climate an element in their make-up also.

The Ticino is called after its river, and down from the Alps tumble the lesser waters of the Ticinese valleys: the Maggia, the Formazza, the Centovalli, the Onsernone, the Vergeletto, the Verzasca. Named and unnamed, there are hundreds of others — torrents that calm themselves on their way or are occasionally diverted into dams. On summer Saturdays in the Valle Verzasca leather-wrapped motorcyclists thunder dangerously round the bends at Gordola and Vogorno; bearded Germans unload their brightly-coloured rubber canoes at Motta or Brione; stockinged walkers escape to the waterfalls and the woods from their orderly city worlds. And the tiny hillside village of Corippo dies a little more.

Corippo dies because its true inhabitants are old. The red-haired postmistress is young; her children are children, but they and their contemporaries are a small minority. In the world of today there is no reason for this village, for its steeply sloped meadows cut with scythe and hook, its rough, narrow pathways instead of streets, its rank nettlebeds and manure heaps, its odour of hay in June. Like medieval cells, its cramped houses jostle for breathing space; cobbled passages lead nowhere; doors open into hovel kitchens. All day long the tourists gaze in wonder at the past, cameras recording an ancient barn or red hens pecking. Two old men, slippered and silent, make their slow way down to the roadside graveyard, sticks poking out a safe path on the stony surface. The graveyard's nearly full — with the Arcotti family mainly, and the Scetrinis, but there's room for a couple more. The old men want it to be them; they want to be among their friends again. They turn and creep back together, thinking that one will outlive the other and wondering which, and why.

Corippo has a mayor, Signora Arcotti. She, too, is old and has seen the changes, seen the withering begin and seen it spread. Summer visitors have the better houses, coming for a while, then folding over the wooden shutters until next year. There are public lavatories and a telephone now, but the only shop sells no more than it ever did: ice-creams and films and Mars bars. The inn is modest.

The church bell at Corippo chimes out the time on the hour and the half-hour, repeating itself a moment later in the manner of the Alps. It chimes, as well, when something's the matter; and at ten past eight every morning, except Sundays and *giorni festivi*, to mark the arrival of the baker. On Fridays the big orange Migros van offers groceries and vegetables and meat to the *haus fraus* of Zürich and St Gallen. The elderly locals don't buy much.

Sparkling granite is sawn into long slabs for gravestones and tabletops; into smaller ones for paving and roofing; into blocks for kerbs and walls; into posts and supports for pergolas. The rock of the river, or bare on the mountainside, is tinged with pink. Rock shapes the landscape, is wrestled with and respected: Switzerland's roots. The rock beneath the twisting road to Corippo cracked and slipped away in the summer of 1987; more avalanches, every winter, tumble more boulders into the torrents.

Birches and larches, oak and maple and chestnut, soften this intimidating, ubiquitous stone. They grow in crevices and on slopes, sprouting miraculously, cut away from sudden little plains where goats graze and cow-bells rattle. In May the crickets chirp, a chorus of thousands in meadows brightened with cornflowers and campions and field geraniums. In June a wind gets up; a pale sea ripples through the mountain greenery as the underside of ash and birch leaf stakes its modest claim; obediently, trunks sway; high, slender branches bend. Tranquil an hour ago, the sky is wispy with shreds of cloud; and then is threatening. Wide open to the hillside, the west doors of the church at Frasco creak on their hinges. Raindrops spatter the Stations of the Cross. If the river rises, the Bailey bridge at Gerra is not inviting.

In August it's cool in the Valle Verzasca by five. There's half a day of sunshine, morning or evening, depending on where you are and how the mountains cast their shadows. On a *wanderweg* near Brione pots of the season's jam are laid out on a bench, for sale: take one and leave the money, no one steals in Switzerland. In the little inn at Froda there's *trota al burro* and *patate* with rosemary, and purple, pungent Merlot, Froda's own Selezione d'Ottobre. In the inn at Sonogno the walkers crowd around a photograph of the first car in the valley, wooden spokes and solid tyres, 1904. At Sonogno the handicapped line up in wheelchairs for their downhill race. Plying back and forth since dawn, a helicopter takes food and wine and passengers to the heights of Mount Ephra, where a bishop will bless the refuge at midday. Business is brisk at the pizzeria at Piee.

The post-bus drivers rule the valley. Some eventually move on, or away; others are themselves of the valley, familiar faces year after year. They are peremptory with the cars they meet on the narrow sections of the road, firmly commanding that they reverse, indicating the cliff edge to which they should draw in. In the mornings, going down, there is the clamour of schoolchildren, and then up come the walkers and the climbers — the Swiss, the Germans, the French, the Dutch, young and old, in groups and in families, alone or in couples. Some make the journey in order to stroll, to picnic by the river, lazily to lunch in Lavertezzo. Laden with tents and bed-rolls, others head for the mountain passes, over the top to the Maggia, the trek to San Gottardo. The yellow post-buses were once the valley's lifeline, and often still are. The careless walker who is a second or so late for the eighteen thirty-five at Sonogno is at Sonogno until the morning.

Tourism is as vital here as it is among the lakes below. In the valley, and in Switzerland, commerce dictates that of necessity there must be a bright side: everything works both ways. Without the rain the grass that makes the butter won't thrive; without the breathless July heat the grapes won't ripen. The cars and motorcycles that disturb the valley's peace ensure that its inns are comfortable. Derelict barns and sheep-shelters have been made into snug *rustici* by newcomers from outside the region. 'We should be sad to see it,' a local woman says, but adds that, as they were, the ruins were no use to anyone. Time was, she adds also, when the new little supermarket was not there, nor the valley's only bank.

Time was, too, when the post-bus drivers did not speak French and German as effortlessly as Italian. Time was when lone climbers perished instead of being rescued from the air. But the snows still come when the valley belongs to itself again, and its pretty wild-flowered habitat is still fearsome in its less friendly seasons. Old peasant women still labour on the slopes beside their men, and turn the dung, and milk the cows. The valley's genius is Switzerland's own: a genius for taking everything in its stride, for making the most of what is there. When the old ways die hard it is because the new ones are not, economically, within reach.

The roadside telephones that always work, the reliable post, the accurate clocks, are no mere expressions of national pride: communication matters here. Efficiency is a weapon in the compromise with the mountains that are ultimately always in command; only human ingenuity, only calm precision and co-operation, can exact from their indomitable bleakness a *modus vivendi*. Sentiment is not bred in the Valle Verzasca, nor doubt and suspicion about change. These are the luxuries of a softer world.

(1991)

Journey to Suburbia

'D AMN!' SHE SAID when she was old, on discovering there wasn't another packet of potato crisps. She added a handful of cornflakes to the plate of cold meat she had prepared for her husband, in the hope that he wouldn't be able to tell the difference. She loved the theatre, novels and the wireless, breakfast in bed and sitting in the sun. All household matters were tedious.

Photographs taken eighty years ago show a child with long dark hair and solemn eyes. On a Swiss ski slope a slight girl — already beautiful — smiles shyly. More confident, she is elusive on the promenade at Montreux, a movement of her head impatiently blurring the camera's impertinence.

This is an appallingly dull place, she wrote of Wimereux in 1909. She was sixteen then, trailing round the resort hotels of Europe with her mother and her older, more sophisticated sister. Her most intimate friend was her journal, to which she confided a whole adolescent cagmag — as she would say — of secrets, comments, and opinions.

Wimereux, August 6th. Edith was talking to me today about getting married. She says she would do it if she met a man rich enough, but it wasn't worth marrying just for a home etc. unless one did it really well; and then she added that she had never met a really rich eligible man. But she doesn't seem inclined to go the whole hog, as Aunt Matilda did, and marry a person she hated.

They were upper-class Anglo-Indians, displaced by the death of the girls' father. They passed their time reading, writing letters, wondering about the future, and observing their fellow hotel-guests.

Lausanne, September 1st. There is a most amusing trio staying here, a husband, a wife and a bow-wow. The husband has grey hair and nice absent eyes. The wife has a plain face, what she considers a fascinating giggle, and lovely golden hair (all her own). The bow-wow's hair is dark and barber's blocky. He has a horridly affected way of speaking, and the wife and he are so affectionate. The husband takes it all quite calmly. If he were not married I should say he was on the way to being super.

The slang of the Raj flavours every page. There are doubts and speculations, uncertainty about the future. Should they return to India, or settle for England now? What would living in a suburb be like? Should they simply continue to traipse about the Continent?

Venice, September 13th. Edith was saying the other day how abstract subjects have come back into fashion for conversation between men and girls. In Mother's day, girls had no idea of conversation with a man beyond flirting, and certainly that can hardly rank as an abstract subject. Yet it seems to me that flirting is as much a test of a man's decentness as evening clothes are supposed to be of his appearance.

Letters arrive from Geoffrey and Gordon and Stanley and Wilfrid (*Poor camel, he has failed his exam*). Bicard has been gone on somebody for as long as ten years. Charlie has had bad luck in a briefer romance. Marriage does not seem easy: a stupid wife believes blindly in her husband's virtues, a clever one notices his coarseness and unreasonableness. But there was spirit enough for whatever game of chance had to be played. *I want to grow up as quickly as ever I can. I want to have great fun.*

She intends to enjoy herself a good deal more than her sister did at the same age in India. She sees no reason not to try at least, instead of envying other people. *Emerson says envy is ignorance. He really isn't bad in places, Emerson.*

September 11th. My birthday and I'm seventeen. 'A day's march nearer home,' as the hymn says, in my case 'home' meaning my twenty-first birthday. On this day last year I was at Knokke, the year before in Cornwall, the year before at Quesnoy, in a convent! Thirteen, twelve, eleven; I had my tenth crossing back from the Ardennes, and my ninth I've forgotten. I was at Crowborough for my eighth; my seventh and sixth were in India. My fifth I remember perfectly. It was at the Naini Tal and I had a party at which I behaved so disgracefully that half my presents were confiscated. My first, of course, was in India.

November 1st. I have been gleaning many Anglo-Indian customs I did not know from Edith. It appears that at every dance a certain number of sitting-out places are arranged in more than semi-darkness. They are called Kala Juggers (black holes) and it is quite an understood thing for men to take girls who like that sort of thing into one, where they remain for sometimes two or three dances and hold hands etc. Only once, Edith told me, a man suggested to her to go into one, but she replied that she didn't see the fun of sitting in a black hole holding hands.

At Montana, on January 8th 1910, Mr Rogers turns up.

Mr Rogers was in the army for seven years. Once he blew himself up. He must have been so fine-looking; he is tall, with a ripping figure, but one side of his face is blackened. Since then he has been in a workshop near Paris. He must train there for two years in order to become an electrical engineer. Mr Rogers is now twenty-five, a most original and amusing person. India and the army haven't spoilt him a bit.

February 4th. I've had a letter from Mr Rogers. He has had an exhilarating time in the deluge in Paris. He had to escape from his room in the middle of the night, leaving all his clothes behind . . . He was in his element, saving a man from drowning in the Seine and doing salvage work. He has a brain, that man, and a wonderful command of the English language.

Mr Rogers writes to Rome and to Verona, his further exploits modestly recounted. A Major Riddell intervenes, being on the spot, but he doesn't entirely come up to scratch. *Danced twice with Major Riddell. He is one of those men who does everything beautifully, has delightful manners and good looks, and yet is quite a useless member of the community.*

From Lucerne there's a trip to the Rigi. *A lovely air up there, but an ugly bare place. A Polytechnic party went up in the same funicular, such an amusing lot, I was glad we hadn't missed them. Everything of importance was referred to a Mr Rogers (!) who was personally conducting them . . . Incidentally, I've just had a letter from the real Mr Rogers, who says I must count myself a friend for life from this date.*

But somehow or other the real Mr Rogers fades away. Back in Lausanne again, Montana is a 'misty dream'. Mr Rogers thinks of Switzerland for his Easter holidays, but changes his mind and doesn't come. *I feel that I hate Lausanne with its ugly, clean houses and streets. At present I can take no pleasure in seeing the lake even.*

From Switzerland Edith returns to India. *She looked so absurdly young as she squeezed my hand and gazed tearfully out of the railway window. She will be very changed when I see her again, I expect, perhaps married and beyond the stage of tearfulness. Edith really likes men very much and makes distinct efforts to attract them . . . Dear me, I would rather be able to write decently than most other things in the world. If one could choose, say, between an ordinary so-called happy marriage, with plenty of children and moderate means, or being a really clever writer, I would not hesitate for an instant. Not I!*

I met her forty years later, a tiny woman in the English suburbs the sisters had wondered about. The wit and perception that were being sharpened in her girlhood journal had mellowed, but the edge of neither was entirely gone. She had come to terms with the suburb and with marriage, with wars and death, and the funless austerity of the England of that time. She no longer kept a journal. She didn't much bother with herself any more. Once she had danced in the Hammersmith Palais with T.S. Eliot, but she didn't tell me to impress. During the years between India and the suburb where she found herself now it was just something amusing that had happened. Soon afterwards she married the first unsuitable man.

An unobtrusive privacy replaced the eagerness to enjoy that runs through her diary. All sorts of other things had happened, but she did not touch upon them. A chasm separated the woman from the child and the girl, but I was not aware of it because I did not then know about the other person she had been. The survival kit didn't show. There were no regrets, no words of disappointment, only nicely judged gossip and warmth. The confident anticipation that bubbles through the pages I later read had been transformed into qualities more suited to middle age: her kindness was extraordinary, her modesty attractive, her sympathy rare. 'Amusing' was still her favourite word, and there were traces of the beauty she had once considered not to be a camera's business. Nor had the style of the girl who thought Emerson not bad in places been lost. In the first moment of meeting her I knew she was a singular woman: if she hadn't had great fun herself, she saw no reason to lose faith in it for everyone else.

(1986)

Eldorado

A T THAT TIME there was a holocaust without fire: an airy hell on plains and hillsides before starvation made a welcome deathbed of ditches and of hearths. The summer of 1845, the summer of 1846, and the grim seasons that followed: the great hunger that came like a plague to Ireland stacked the odds against survival and went on doing so until 1849. And the harshest irony among many was that even though the hunger so efficiently gathered in its human harvest, it left too many behind: the little farms, knocked sideways by misfortune, were unable to sustain the poor relations who temporarily huddled around them, those whose single other hope was to board the coffin ships to America.

Against such a background — as in legend that tells of wonders — there magically was talk of gold. The metal, almost entirely unseen, had for centuries been a talking point: a wonder that neither rusted nor tarnished, was so soft it could be delicately worked yet did not wear away, so rare it could be effortlessly traded. Once upon a time the high-king Malachy had acquired a greater stature when he wore the gold he won from the proud invader; whole armies of warriors had fought for its chalices and its masks. It was the setting for the jewels of queens, a gift brought to the Christ child, the panacea for all distress.

For as long as anyone could remember, tales had been told of lake-pebbles transformed by fairy power into nuggets, of golden threads gleaming through the ripples of a stream, of gold in the gills of fishes, gold laid by geese, gold flashing in the eyes of swans. But the tales told now were different. This was no mockery at the end of a rainbow, but facts you could believe in without an effort, offered as if in apology for the ugly years there had been, the fair due of a victim people. From the ports of Europe began the rush to the hills of California; from the ports of Ireland began the journey of those who had suffered more than most.

More and more of them had begun to reject the last chance offered by those ill-fated coffin ships, almost a quarter of whose voyagers perished on the Atlantic. Those whom the small farms could not provide for had at least survived, and luck does not strike twice: better surely to remain, to hang on somehow, to walk the roads if need be. But an Eldorado had not been there when that philosophy seemed sensible; an Eldorado had not offered the protection of its inspiration, this glimpse of heaven from a landscape that not long ago was hell's. And so they went, family savings borrowed for the price of a ticket, blessed by their priests, their own prayers to the Virgin nourishing expectation. Some took a wife and children, and the old when they would not be left. A dream spread its net, as the Famine had.

They died in their thousands. Some reached the Mission Dolores in San Francisco and are there today, beneath their stones: Ryans and Callaghans, Coffees and Littles and Byrnes. Silent now in that tranquil place are the accents of Cork and Meath, Carlow and Waterford and Tipperary.

★

In 1848, when James Marshall discovered gold in the American River, San Francisco was little more than a village settlement. Within months an army of almost a hundred thousand prospectors was on its way: the forty-niners — called after the succeeding year, since it took most of them the best part of that time to reach a destination that was farther than they'd bargained for. What none of them knew was that even if they were never to find the yellow lumps they sought, their presence was destined to bring a boom of riches to the scattering of natives. The Mormon, Sam Brannan, already commercially active in the area and now supplying the newcomers with food and shovels and pick-axes, became San Francisco's first bonanza king. A tent city sprang up on the way to the fabled hills, and such sharp-witted entrepreneurs as Brannan continued to offer it all it needed. Americans constituted half of this travelling multitude; the Irish came next, then British, Italians, Poles, Swiss, Dutch, Swedes, French, Germans, Belgians, Hispanics, Hawaiians, Chinese — people from everywhere.

When the surface gold gave out in 1849 some moved on to try again, their only common currency a distrust of one another. Others gave up and returned to San Francisco. The English bucks decided to remain there, becoming card-sharpers or old-style businessmen toting insurance; the Dutch adventurers turned respectable; the Swedes were restless before they settled; most of those who wanted to found a niche. Few of the Famine Irish returned to Ireland, knowing there wasn't much point, and the new San Francisco — houses replacing the pioneer tents — became their home, too. The city burnt and was rebuilt, and burnt again. Labour was needed. The Irish supplied a lot of it.

★

As the last of the prospectors trickled back from the hills and endeavoured to resell their shovels to Sam Brannan, only a few might have guessed that the cosmopolitan flavour of the migration they'd taken part in was destined to give a city of the future its character. A hundred years on, immigrants were still reaching these few square miles of America, to be absorbed and even honoured: O'Farrell Street, Daly City, Kearny Street, Russian Hill, El Camino Real, Turk Street. Today, Italians serve *pesto* as subtle as any you'll find in Genoa; Greeks make lemon soup and *ghofária plaki*. In orderly hordes, the Chinese perform early-morning gymnastics, their *tai chi* movements as elegant as dancers'. Shamrock flies in for St Patrick's Day. Shillelaghs and hurley sticks are not unknown.

Few modern cities are as attractive as San Francisco, few as invigorating. The mists lift and it stands there in its elegance and its excitement, engendering affection in the briefest of its visitors. The best city on earth, Dylan Thomas called it; Mark Twain gloried in its future.

> This straggling town shall be a vast metropolis: this sparsely populated land shall become a crowded hive of busy men: your waste places shall blossom like the rose and your deserted hills and valleys shall yield bread and wine for unnumbered thousands: railroads shall be spread hither and thither and carry the invigorating blood of commerce to regions that are languishing now: mills and workshops, yea, and *factories* shall spring up everywhere, the mines that have neither name nor place to-day shall dazzle the world with their affluence . . .

City of earthquakes — conceived on a barren waste, born out of honky-tonk wedlock, bums and shady ladies its godparents — it took its chances and ended rich. In its mean backyards hope became ambition, opportunity spelt escape. Nothing else helped this city flourish. It clawed its way to the pretty painted porches of Pacific Heights and the downtown skyscrapers of Market Street. It tamed its Barbary Coast. It built its Alcatraz.

Today it takes the rough with the smooth because it always has, and it accepts as readily as it rejects. No smoking in public places, it insists, while tolerating a legion of deviants; and it doesn't dwell on what its earthy city fathers might have made of that. Among the mannequin yuppies the happy flower children are wrinklies now, and grey old beats caress their ancient bikes. In Japantown the Japanese hurry through clean white sunshine to church. In Cow Hollow, teenagers put their feet up for mid-morning milkshakes — descendants of the Famine Irish or Germans or English bucks, it doesn't matter. Gripmen work the cable cars; if you stroll, you're offered a sidewalk spinal examination, or the fastest-anywhere tattoo, or laser foot surgery.

The Condour — Big Al's Totally Nude — is closed for reconstruction, but only a few blocks away the Pagoda is showing an old favourite, a tale of love in a Peking suburb. A Café Walk begins at Sea Cliff, a Heritage Walk at North Beach. There are visits to the Boxing Museum, to the Lawrence Hall of Science, to the Museum of Ophthalmology. 'Jimmy, gimme, gimme, gimme!' is a hustler's hopeful plea, and 'Bruce, turn out your loose!' and 'Dollar bill, Will?' *Best damn dog we ever had*, says the memorial stone in the Presidio cemetery, and *Here lie our beloved rats*: dear Chocolate and dear Candy.

A hog is exercised in Berkeley. On Fisherman's Wharf a tired old terrier wears glasses. A Santa Claus in shorts crosses Union Square. In the early evening a saxophone duet carries all the way up Vallejo Street Stairs, the air turned balmy now, the music mournful. 'Eight fifty,' the pig-tailed taxi-driver murmurs on Broadway, folding a tourist's twenty-dollar bill, smiling away the change. In Portsmouth Plaza the Mahjong boards are still out. In Haight-Ashbury two men talk about marrying one another.

Creative Divorce, offers a leaflet pressed into the hands of passers-by in Golden Gate Avenue. And by similar means Norman Wilner, director of the Institute for Creative Writing, tells the interested that a student has been paid $12,000 for a travel book, that another sold a short story for $500. Writing is fun, Mr Wilner maintains, and it's a therapy and it's lucrative. *Keeping a journal diary? Learn to sell it! Conquer writer's block!* Mr Wilner in his spare time alone has made $100,000, and stories are everywhere.

A Santa Claus in shorts is surely one. A Mrs Ozick, already into afternoon highballs, her tears shed earlier on to the summer sumach and blueblossom that enrich her shingled mansion, has only to write it all down: he cheated one last time and has gone, leaving her with the Oldsmobile and the house. A boy from Ballinasloe, transgressing the law by remaining beyond the limitation of his temporary work permit, writes to the girl he left behind. *I can't, I'm sorry. If I come back to see you now they'll never let me in again.*

Mrs Coit had a story in her time: Lillie Hitchcock Coit who was trapped in a house on fire and never forgot the firemen who rescued her. Hers is Coit Tower on the top of Telegraph Hill, hers the memorial to the city's brave firemen in Washington Square. She gave whenever she could, and being wealthy she gave a lot. She waved on fire brigades whenever she saw them going about their work. Moist-eyed and loving, she saw them out of sight.

Leland Stanford had a story in his time. So had Charles Crocker. So had Collis Huntington and Mark Hopkins. They're the Big Four who created the Southern Pacific Railway, bringing vast wealth to the city and to themselves. And William C. Ralston claimed to have built more of San Francisco than anyone else. These are the bonanza kings of the 1860s, whose continued commercial flair took over the game of chance the gold rush had been. Some spirit was born then that has never been quenched.

Lillie Coit is buried with them in Woodlawn Memorial Park, her own small eccentricity safely immortalised. Not far away lies the sheriff of Tombstone, Arizona, renowned for his shoot-out at O.K. Corral. And the man who called himself the Emperor of the United States and Protector of Mexico, a Cockney forty-niner, briefly became a bonanza king himself. A beggar in military uniform, his days of affluence long past, he talked himself into the hearts of San Franciscans, who honoured his imperial fantasy with the occasional civic reception and gave him a good grave. Such resting places, and those who reside there, seem a world away from the Mission Dolores and its forgotten dead. But of course they're not. The great and the good, and those who came empty-handed from the rainbow, are at one in the city that glitters as brightly as the gold of its legend.

(1992)

Extraordinary Ladies

T HE DESCRIPTIVE TERM, Anglo-Irish, is simple in its historical implication. It suggests a foothold within the political ascendancy in Ireland, a continuing connection with England, and a preference for the English language and religion. But when the expression relates purely to literature a confusion is introduced.

Writing in the early 1930s, the scholar and short-story writer Daniel Corkery offered an academic definition that has held sway ever since: 'Literature written in English by Irishmen is now known among us as Anglo-Irish literature, while by Irish literature we mean the literature written in the Irish language and that alone.'

It may seem a little odd that Irishmen such as Frank O'Connor, Liam O'Flaherty and James Joyce should be placed in one category as persons and in another as writers. Nor does there seem to be any good reason why the term 'Irish literature' should not be accepted to mean the writing of Irish people in either Irish or English, and the term 'Anglo-Irish literature' be allowed to designate the writing of the Anglo-Irish. But it is not so.

Scribbling away in one drawing-room or another, Edith Oenone Somerville and Violet Martin (who wrote as Martin Ross) were Anglo-Irish both as human beings and as fiction writers. They were rooted in its Big House world; its *mores* and its attitudes were theirs. What they wrote, rather more than what they were, offended Daniel Corkery, and to this day that same offence is regularly given. A dislike of what Corkery called a 'colonial culture' is understandable indeed, but at the same time it cannot be sensibly argued that literature is a national property — that Turgenev, for instance, wrote only 'for Russia' and Ibsen 'for no alien market'. The truth is that art, no matter what its roots, cannot be owned in this way. In the very process of becoming art it also becomes universal.

Somerville and Ross have to be accepted as creatures of their time and class — and if necessary forgiven for it. They can be accused of presenting the quaintness of Irish life as an Irish joke, of patronising the lower orders by imitating their speech and exposing their foibles. It is true that, like Dickens, they did so affectionately and without sarcasm, but Dickens shared his Englishness with Joe Gargery and Sam Weller as much as he did with Miss Havisham and Lady Tippens. Somerville and Ross, although they considered themselves totally Irish, were on trickier terrain.

Edith Somerville was born in 1858 on the island of Corfu, where her father commanded the 3rd Buffs. When his active military life ended Colonel Thomas Somerville came to live at Drishane in Castle-townshend, West Cork — a house and a place associated ever since with the literary talent of his daughter.

Violet, Edith's cousin and four years younger, came of similar stock in Co. Galway. An ancestor had helped Strongbow to invade Ireland, was granted an estate near Oughterard, and went crusading with Richard Cœur de Lion. In 1777 Ross House, taking its title from the nearby lake, was built where a Martin castle had once stood. When the possibility that Violet's name might appear in print was first mooted it was decided by the family that 'Martin Ross' was a more suitable form for it to take.

Edith was an extrovert, lighthearted girl who loved dogs, enjoyed riding, and painted a bit. Violet, short-sighted and more intense, often permitted a sadness to still her neat, handsome features. The famous collaboration began, not with words on paper nor even stories exchanged, but when Edith painted Violet's portrait in 1886. Attired for the hunting field, Violet perches on the edge of a chair, unsmiling, spectacles dangling, a little melancholy. It isn't difficult to imagine the bustling Edith, hair pinned up, glancing back and forth from canvas to model, chattering, or muttering to herself. Slowly they became friends, and out of the warmth that developed came everything else.

Writing is a solitary business, and to writers who have not engaged in it collaboration is sometimes not easy to understand. 'Our work was done conversationally,' Edith has explained. 'One or the other — not infrequently both simultaneously — would state a proposition. This would be argued, combated perhaps, approved or modified; it would be written down by the (wholly fortuitous) holder of the pen, would be scratched out, scribbled in again.' It is probably true that Violet supplied the sombre tones and the subtler intricacies of plotting, that somewhere in her contribution lay the genius of the partnership. But it is as easy to believe that nothing would have surfaced as completely and as felicitously without Edith's corresponding view of the same scenes and characters, and her meticulous scrutiny of all they invented. The cousins were two halves of a whole, quibbling and enthusing, sharing amazement and delight, and what now reads like unalloyed snobbery — two women, one writer. When Violet died Edith continued as if this separation had not occurred, believing in fact that she still received her cousin's guidance and inspiration.

Edith loved Violet in the possessive, passionate manner that caused Ethel Smyth, on a visit to Drishane in 1919, four years after Violet's death, to assume that the pair had been practising lesbians. They had not, of course. As their biographer, Maurice Collis, points out, Violet might have married; Edith would not have cared for the physical attentions of a man. Nor, though, did she care for those of Dame Ethel. The affection that developed between the cousins, more obsessive on Edith's side than on Violet's, found its release in their literary conjunction. For each, in her different way, that was sufficient.

In July 1890, having already published *An Irish Cousin* but still short of funds, they suggested a series of travel articles to the *Ladies' Pictorial*. Edith would illustrate a trip through Connemara which they planned to make in a jennet and trap, hoping for enough amusement and adventure en route to make up a book after the pieces had appeared in the magazine.

'Johnny Flaherty have a nice jinnet,' they were told in Galway. 'She's able to kill any horse on the road.'

Mr Flaherty promised that if they refrained from touching the animal's ears she'd give them no trouble at all, being if anything 'over-anxious for the road'. With this companion — sometimes as eager as her owner declared, but as often reluctant to move in any direction whatsoever — the two set about dawdling through Connemara with their Bath Olivers and their pot of Bovril, their spirit lamp and a folding rubber bath. They were drenched, assaulted by midges, nibbled by fleas, abused by a harridan who didn't like the look of them, made fools of by the jennet. 'Ah, don't be sparin' him that way, ladies,' the natives called out. 'Nourish him wid the whip.'

But from Maam Cross to Recess, by the waters of Inagh and the Pass

of Selruck, their trials were rewarded. Nothing was taken for granted: a dog was never just a dog, a house never just a house, there were no mere passers-by. On a dull day they embellished, for above all else Somerville and Ross are storytellers.

'We did not ask the Widow Joyce if she could take us in. We simply walked into the house and stayed there.'

If inconvenience resulted, the Joyce household took it in its stride. After the widow had prepared and served a meal and the time came for retirement, she apologised for the fact that the family would now have to pass through the guests' bedroom in order to mount to the loft above it. '. . . a procession of Joyces slowly filed up the ladder, headed by the younger sons of the house, and followed by the widow and the daughter.'

In the meantime another procession was forming beneath the bed-clothes. 'It isn't the little bit they ates I begridges them,' mimicked one of the ladies, 'but 'tis the continial thramplin' they keeps up.' And when the fleas quietened, a goose emerged from beneath the bed.

There is no reference to this overnight stay at the Joyce house in the diaries that were kept. Bits and pieces, experienced elsewhere or by others, may have been knocked together, exaggerated to taste. Or the whole episode may be an invention. The book which they later called *Through Connemara in a Governess Cart* is no strict documentary. Its authors' gifts lie elsewhere: their shared ear for dialect, their shared fascination with the peculiar and the extraordinary, their sense of humour and their clear literary style, combine with an insistent imagination to make them what they so uniquely are.

Within their own Big House realm there was a certain isolation, bred of the suspicion that fiction-writers inspire: thrown together in their governess-cart or in the draughty comfort of Drishane, they found the courage to ignore it. And it was isolation again — the very distance that lay between two upper-class women and the Ireland they wrote about — that permitted their talent to breathe and develop. By chance, or accident of birth, they discovered the perspective that art demands.

(1990)

In Their Own Shadows

L ONG BEFORE HE became one, W.B. Yeats played the part of the great poet. Tall, handsome in his heyday, he affected a variety of mannerisms, his innate good sense seeming powerless to control a stronger urge. Of excessive appearance, George Moore called him, a literary fop with 'a long black cloak drooping from his shoulders, a soft black sombrero on his head, a voluminous black silk tie flowing from his collar, loose black trousers dragging untidily over his long, heavy feet'. Moore, who scorned the mincing of words, likened him to a rook and a crane, or 'a great umbrella forgotten by some picnic party'.

These images were complemented by the poet's talk of 'blue manifestations in the Dublin hills', ritual magic, and the Hermetic Order of the Golden Dawn. At the drop of a hat, he retailed details of a nightmare in which he was haunted by a sewing-machine. He claimed to have seen a centaur, and a naked woman shooting an arrow at a star. He lay down in a coffin and solemnly listened to the chiming of bells. A medium, whose control, Nelly, lived in her stomach, advised him to become a yogi priest. Fortunately, he demurred.

Yeats's love of Maud Gonne — in retrospect seeming to be one of the great romances of our time, and all the more so for being one of frustration and folly — is the third element in his personal trinity. Maud Gonne was beautiful, tiresome and a tease, but Yeats's infatuation was so intense and so long-lasting that when her daughter was old enough he resolved that if he couldn't have the mother he would try for the girl. Iseult Gonne rejected him, and in 1917 Yeats more sensibly married George Hyde Lees.

Maud Gonne had been 'the troubling of his life', but this unhappiness spawned many a poem that otherwise would not have seen the light of day. In the same way his obsession with the realm of spirits, and his efforts to link it with his interest in Irish mythology, created the stuff of poetry. It is not the inspiration, he affirmed himself, that's the heart of the matter, but the practical writing of the lines. 'When I had finished I brought it round to my Uncle George Pollexfen, and could hardly read so collapsed I was. It was a kind of vision that beset me day and night. Not that I ever wrote more than a few lines in a day. But those few lines took me hours. And the rest of the time, I walked about the roads thinking of it.'

George Yeats calmed a life in which contradictory elements and emotional muddle were beginning to become disruptive. There was also Yeats's recurring fear that he had inherited a 'nervous weakness' from his mother. 'The feeling is always the same: a consciousness of energy, of certainty, and of transforming power stopped by a wall, by something one must either submit to or rage against helplessly. It often alarms me; is it the root of madness?'

The inquisitive mind of the artist is obliged by its very nature to wander irrationally, wildly, and often foolishly, no matter what the consequences. And art, as Yeats came to observe, is a draining pursuit, both mentally and physically. The toll it takes of the practitioner can leave behind an ordinariness so personally disappointing that some feel drawn towards fanciful disguise. Yeats, who was a shrinkingly shy man and far from unaware of his shortcomings, hid behind useful affectations; and his eccentric forays into the mystic world naturally intensified the impression that he was — before he proved the contrary — a charlatan.

Yet his dourly practical Pollexfen side was always waiting to float to the surface. It did so on the confidence of his later years. The awkward, headstrong youth turned into the thoughtful senator. The inept philanderer came to wonder in a down-to-earth manner if his waning sexuality would affect his poetic drive. The solemn folklore enthusiast read detective stories and Wild West novels. He laughed more, and became a croquet player of inordinate cunning. When he won the Nobel Prize his first question was: 'How much is it worth?' But even so, to the end of his life, Yeats saw apparitions and sought signs and portents in dreams.

★

Sean O'Casey's first employment was as a stock boy in a chandler's. It was the world of genteel, lower-middle-class Protestant Dublin and, even though it was his own world, he didn't like it. Later he became a labourer on the Great Northern Railway and remained there for nine years. It suited him better: he was a Protestant among Catholics, proud, rigid and idealistic, immediately an outsider. Instead of lingering jollily in public houses, he wrote political pamphlets and songs, became Secretary of the Irish Citizen Army and a founder member of the Irish Labour Party. In Dublin parlance he was 'a quare fella'.

He also wrote plays. They weren't very good and when he sent them to the Abbey Theatre the distinguished directors patted him on the head but returned the plays. O'Casey, in his workman's boots and revolutionary's trenchcoat, bristled each time it happened. Then he wrote *The Shadow of a Gunman* and everything changed.

The boots and the trenchcoat were now in the stalls, Lady Gregory on one side of them, W.B. Yeats on the other. Lennox Robinson hovered solicitously near by. When *Juno and the Paycock* was staged it was apparent — as it has been ever since — that this oddity from the back streets was touched with genius. *The Plough and the Stars* caused riots, always a good sign in Dublin.

There followed O'Casey's legendary quarrel with Yeats and with Ireland, his exile, his baiting of the Irish Catholic Church and the English literary establishment, his communism, his marriage, his friendship with the Shaws and with Harold Macmillan, his domesticity in Devon. Politically naïve and wildly disputatious, he relished a fight and thrived on failure and on fury. He was also an exception to a literary rule: it does not often happen that art tumbles out of narcissism. In O'Casey, the man and the writer were related to an unusual degree.

His strength was fiction, and in their pursuit of truth writers of fiction often supply their own interpretation of reality. The four years he subtracted from his age, the chronological muddle of his autobiography, his role as a cuckold in marriage, his enemies' point of view, were all coloured by O'Casey's view of himself. And often his hothead's indignation was justified. The rejection of *The Drums of Father Ned* by the Dublin Festival in 1958 seemed outrageous at the time, and revived sympathy for O'Casey in Ireland. James Agate's shabby private little censorship — his veiled threat of a drubbing that prevented the staging of *Purple Dust* — was an act of monumental meanness. O'Casey played the victim with some justification. And long before young men were fashionably angry he unleashed a fury that in the end burnt out his talent. But not before it had done what he asked of it.

★

'If it begins to mean something,' Samuel Beckett wrote, 'I can't help it.' He referred to the mystery of existence, to the human condition, to his own place in the endlessness of time. 'I have passed by here, this has passed by me, thousands of times, its turn has come again, it will pass on and something else will be there, another instant . . .'

One stormy March night, walking on the East Pier at Dun Laoghaire, he realised that meanings did not interest him. He was aware of a revelation that presented him with 'the whole thing. The turning point, at last. This, I imagine, is what I have chiefly to set down this evening, against the day when my work will be done and perhaps no place in my memory, and no thankfulness, for the miracle — for the fire that set it alight. What I saw was . . . that the dark I have struggled to keep at bay is in reality my most valuable —'

In that early version of *Krapp's Last Tape* the machine is abruptly turned off, but on the pier the anemometer continues to spin like a propeller in the wind. Bursts of foam are caught in the swivelling beam of the lighthouse, and the man who went out for a walk is left with a 'strange association of storm and night with the light of understanding'.

It had not before occurred to Beckett, as it instinctively does to many writers of fiction, that the truth offered by storytellers derives its potency from the unique nature of the human apparatus that has gathered it, and perhaps is best left at that. His intellectualism and severity had blocked from him the simple fact that his own introspections constituted the roots of the art he sought to express. Academic success at Trinity College, Dublin, and endeavours to translate *Finnegans Wake* into French belonged to the more ordinary side of him, in company with skill at bridge and cricket.

Real people and real places got him going. *Waiting for Godot* belongs in the Dublin mountains, where he walked so regularly and knew so well. The Elsner sisters, Beckett's kindergarten teachers in the suburb of Foxrock near Dublin, occur in *Molloy* exactly as they were in life, with their cook Hannah and their dog Zulu. The postman who every morning approached the Becketts' pleasant villa whistling *The Roses are Blooming in Picardy* — that 'unforgettable banquet of music' — makes more than one fictional appearance. Foxrock railway station is the railway station in *All That Fall* and *Watt*.

He wants a ticket to the end of the line, cried Mr Nolan.

Is it a white man? said Lady McCann.

Which end? said Mr Gorman.

What end? said Mr Nolan.

Watt did not reply.

The round end or the square end? said Mr Nolan.

The Slow and Easy that line was called. Harcourt Street terminus was a turntable; the Bray terminus was, more squarely, just an end. The journey, so often taken in Beckett's childhood, remains meticulously charted. The likeness of Thomas Farrell, stationmaster of that time, is not forgotten, nor the diploma he won in the Station Improvement Scheme. But there is hardly any doubt that in some other place, with different recollections, Beckett would have succeeded as well.

His memory, and what he does with it, is what matters: his bewilderment, his affection for people or places, his chattily remarking to his mother when he was four that the sky must be further away than it seemed. Irritated by the observation for some reason of her own, she tartly replies in *Malone Dies*, 'It is as precisely as far away as it appears to be.' In *Company* she displays even greater annoyance. In *The End* she snaps, 'Fuck off.'

★

In his book, *Four Dubliners* — originally a series of lectures — Richard Ellmann drops O'Casey and brings in Wilde and Joyce to make up his foursome with Yeats and Beckett. At first glance the quartet have in common only the accident of their birth in a city they chose not to linger in. All four of them packed their bags in their early twenties, Joyce and Beckett hastening to Paris, Wilde to Oxford, Yeats to London. 'The geographical change', observes Ellmann, 'symbolized . . . an attempt to proceed from the known to the unknown, to remake themselves in unfamiliar air.'

Remake themselves they did. Wilde 'planted a few orchids' instead of the usual wild oats, and set about establishing himself as the sexually and religiously ambivalent figure that shadowed him for the rest of his life. He also sharpened his wit on those university pedagogues who were foolish enough to bother him with their attentions. Required as a punishment to construe from the Greek the beginning of St Matthew's

182

version of Christ's betrayal, he insisted on continuing to the end of the episode. 'Let us proceed,' was how he put it, 'and see what happened to the unfortunate man.'

Yeats — rarely given to such throwaway stuff — entered what he himself called his 'second puberty'. When he was sixty-eight he not surprisingly felt that his sexual powers were diminishing. 'I have as healthy flesh and blood as any rhymer's had,' he'd proudly noted sixteen years earlier, and he rather missed the departure of all that. He underwent a vasectomy, an operation performed at that time by an Austrian physiologist, Eugen Steinach, who peddled the theory that rejuvenation would follow. It appeared not to do so, but the poet's versemaking — always associated in his mind with lovemaking — was injected with fresh vigour. So at least Yeats believed: self-delusion plays a greater part in the emergence of art than is ever allowed.

Earlier, Joyce had experienced another problem. Having created a cuckold, he wondered how it felt to be one. 'Jim wants me to go with other men,' his wife reported, 'so that he will have something to write about.' She didn't greatly care for the idea and in the end was prepared to do no more for the cause of twentieth-century literature than address him in a note as 'Dear Cuckold'. This appeared to do the trick.

Understandably, Joyce himself was less hesitant in the same cause. Having arranged for Leopold Bloom to ogle Gerty MacDowell by the Dublin seaside, he set about tasting the experience afresh for himself. In Switzerland, Gerty's finely veined hands were borrowed from a young woman doctor he attempted to court by plying her with obscene letters he was confident would interest her. In fact they startled her beyond measure and he was obliged to turn his attention to Marthe Fleischmann, whom he chanced to observe through a poorly curtained lavatory window. Marthe Fleischmann had a limp: Gerty MacDowell acquired one.

Joyce was a self-styled poseur who saw no reason not to disguise in whatever way he could the 'poor silly boy' who shared the same body with the writer of genius. That same silly boy is to be found in many of the extravagances of Wilde and Yeats, and in O'Casey's hotheadedness. Only Beckett sends him packing. Yet Beckett belongs with his eminent predecessors, and not just because he happens to be Irish and a writer: Richard Ellmann convincingly relates Beckett's voice to theirs, showing, for instance, how much his 'anxious alleycrawlers' have in common with

Wilde's insouciant boulevardiers. He demonstrates also that however unlike Beckett these predecessors were, 'at least some of their interests appear to be proleptic of his. Qualities in his predecessors which had previously been less conspicuous he pushes to the fore.'

But never for Beckett the green carnation, nor blue manifestations, nor noisy complaint, nor teasing mischievousness. Four of these literary Dubliners ensured that posterity had a place for them by attending, even unconsciously, to their images. The fifth didn't care: Beckett's grim visage and grey cropped head, his remembered humanity as a Red Cross worker in France during the Second World War, comprise what outward show there is. And if he'd had his way there wouldn't even be that.

(1988)

Old Fusty

'WHO IS William Gerhardie?' I remember enquiring in a London pub some time in the late nineteen fifties. Some old fusty, came the reply, who had incarcerated himself in a flat behind Broadcasting House because no one read his novels any more. 'A genius', was another suggestion, put forward without much conviction.

William Gerhardie was born in 1895 in St Petersburg. The Gerhardie family, of German origin, had settled in England and later made their way to Russia, where they had established a successful cotton business. *The Polyglots* is the title of Gerhardie's best known novel; *Memoirs of a Polyglot* that of his autobiography. The repetition of the word reflects the cosmopolitan flavour of the Gerhardie family life, and the odd blend of commerce and culture that often surfaced in Gerhardie himself. He once attempted to patent a disposable self-pasting toothbrush.

Thus, for me at least, William Gerhardie might have died had it not been for his biographer, Dido Davies, who turned his life into one of the most fascinating chronicles of its kind. Literary biographers often make the mistake of choosing the wrong subject. A novelist — or any artist — admired for what he produces, may not necessarily have lived anything but the most mundane of lives. As Proust pointed out, to prefer the person to his books is to prefer the second-best. Yet in choosing to write the life of William Gerhardie, Dido Davies chose well. His story is a good one, not because of what he wrote but because of what he was.

When young, he was precocious. Still in his teens, he was dispatched to England to learn something of the business world, but he decided he didn't care for it and in 1915 enlisted instead. Although inept as a soldier, when the war ended he found himself a valued member of the British Military Mission in Siberia, which was currently meddling in post-Revolution Russia. To warn the rest of the world of the dangers of Bolshevism, he was sent on a far-ranging propaganda exercise, and ended by being awarded the OBE. He was twenty-four.

The family were now living in Bolton, the considerable wealth of the St Petersburg days all gone. Encouraged by his mother, as he was in all his endeavours, Gerhardie decided he was a young man destined not to go unnoticed. If an intellectual with a foreign name could make his way in the British army he could surely make it anywhere. He began with Oxford, and settled down to write a novel.

For the rest of his life the lure of the limelight nagged him. It was his inspiration and his tormentor; it nourished the seeds of his destruction. Gerhardie was vain to an almost painful degree, egocentric to an absurd one. He was ravenous for praise, fearful of even a hint of criticism. Other writers of the time, sensing the considerable promise of his novels as soon as they appeared, were generous. But this generosity is noticeably most lavish when Gerhardie himself reports it. 'What do I hear? Gerhardie? The very man I always wanted to meet,' cooed H.G. Wells. 'You're a genius,' pronounced Shaw. Arnold Bennett raved, as did D.H. Lawrence and Katherine Mansfield. Gerhardie maintained he'd heard that Evelyn Waugh was envious, and went on to quote Waugh as declaring, 'I know I have great talent, but he has genius.'

If Gerhardie gilded this particular lily, he certainly didn't need to. He was hugely admired, a writer's writer if ever there was one, his voice as individual as any of those that drew attention to his wit and his invention. But more and more he was being hampered by his obsession with self-promotion.

That Gerhardie fell into the newspaper magnate's clutches is typical of both men. Beaverbrook could offer the adrenalin of publicity, and was himself on the look-out for the new and the different. Having decided to make Gerhardie his boy, he spread him around the Establishment and plastered him all over his newspapers. 'A splendid failure,' he grandiloquently designated him when, eventually, he decided his protégé couldn't be rammed down the throats of the British novel-reading public. From fawning appreciatively on the great man, Gerhardie turned to begging for tit-bits, but Beaverbrook's cupboard had a way of being cruelly empty when he realised he'd made a mistake.

The pursuit of fame was very nearly matched by the pursuit of women. Their bodies interested Gerhardie rather more than their minds, and he made no bones about it. Yet they bent over backwards for him (or forwards when the occasion called for their chastisement, as regularly it did). Briefly pondering the notion of marriage to the widow of an American razor-blade king, he confided to his mother that the thought of having 'to go slow where other women were concerned is too disheartening for a man of my versatility'. His mother quite agreed.

Besides being a womaniser, Gerhardie is good value because once he'd stopped falling on his feet his misadventures were increasingly comic. Lecturing in America on 'Love and Literature', his failure to move his audiences turned the experience into a nightmare. On one occasion 'I suddenly felt it was very cruel, very unjust of these red-faced men in ill-fitting clothes to recline in their chairs . . . while I had to stand and apparently speak. I wanted to cry.' The situation worsened when the same ill-clad men declared his 'Love and Literature' dreary and demanded that he lecture them on the Boy Scout Movement instead.

As suddenly as he had once decided that he intended to be noticed, Gerhardie gave up. He retired to his flat in Hallam Street, abandoning the dream of occupying a privileged position in a 'small harem' in his middle age. Having exhausted the rôles of Brilliant Young Novelist and Anglo-Russian Eccentric, he settled now for that of Author with Work in Progress. He was not a recluse. Long telephone conversations, sometimes of five or six hours, were conducted. Women arrived from time to time to tidy up, and heard about the masterpiece that was under way, a great tetralogy entitled 'The Present Breath'.

But essentially his life in Hallam Street was solitary. He washed his own clothes, studied the *Exchange and Mart* for bargains, wrote to film stars to inform them of their suitability for various parts in his novels, contacted publishers with suggestions for reprints, and theatre managers about dramatisations. He was cold and impoverished. The L.E.B. supplied him with a new electric cooker free of charge because his existing one was so old it was dangerous. In readiness for the limelight that would return one day to claim him, he touched up photographs in which his thinning hair was noticeable. Hoping to jog people's memories, he inserted a notice in *The Times* stating that he had decided to add a final 'e' to his name.

Gerhardie grumbled out a finicky, cantankerous existence until he was eighty-one, unwilling to permit visitors to use his lavatory, disinfecting the coins he received in change. When he died there was no tetralogy, just cardboard cartons full of jottings, and a collection of essays which were later published under the title *God's Fifth Column*. These essays are all that Gerhardie himself was: lively, illuminating, incisive, funny. His novels tend to meander, the essays do not. Rescued from oblivion by his affectionate biographer, he deserves a posthumous saunter in the limelight.

(1990)

With Mr Links in Venice

M R LINKS IS always in Venice. He has made it his city, as surely as Canaletto did, and it isn't difficult to share his point of view.

> It is the Byzantine traces or the gothic building that catch my eye
> and I accept too readily John Ruskin's derision of the High Renaissance
> and what we now call Baroque. Yet, with an inconsistency worthy of
> the great man himself, I am attracted by the painters who chose to
> explore the visible world rather than by those Ruskin himself admired
> for their preoccupation with the sublime and the mystical. Giovanni
> Bellini, Carpaccio or Canaletto will draw me into a church or gallery
> while Titian, Tintoretto or Tiepolo find me still at my coffee when it
> is closing time.

In spring, or August heat, or as the season wanes — when the sunny days shorten and there's even a hint of a chill in the evening air — you'll still find, somewhere, *Venice for Pleasure* by J.G. Links. It is true that on a particular day in November it doesn't accompany Mrs Carole Haye of Beloit, Wisconsin, who is sitting over her coffee at Florian's. It is safe to guess that it is not known to the members of the Czech national orchestra — having a day off between performances in Padua and Bologna — nor to the ninety-odd academics attending a gender conference in a hotel on the Lido. But J.G. Links's master-work is nonetheless in evidence — consulted en route to the Palazzo Querini-Stampalia and en route to the Naval Museum. It has been, the night before, an insomniac's nourishment in the Pensione Seguso; and left in error in the bar of the Gritti Palace.

On this day in November the excitement — for Venetians — is that their city is almost their own again. The Czech national orchestra, the gender people, Mrs Carole Haye and other Mrs Hayes, the schoolchildren out for the day from Mestre, the art groups, the foursomes from Worcestershire and Edinburgh, are nothing compared with the multitudes of summer and spring, when Venice all but bursts its elegant clothing. Every year the city agrees that it will sooner or later have to do something about it: only those who have a smattering of Venetian history — or at least know who St Theodore or Bernardo Bellotto was — should be admitted. Seriously, half humorously, this notion is floated; and dropped, as it always is. But in November no one even mentions the necessity for an entry examination. In November Venice is closing down: there's room for everyone.

Mrs Haye spreads herself at her table at Florian's, one of a hundred on the paving that the sun has not yet reached. Across the square more yellow-clothed tables are added to a similar sprawl at Quadri's, and then the morning music begins: snatches from *Oklahoma* at Quadri's, 'Smoke Gets in Your Eyes' at Florian's.

Across the city, on the Zattere rafts, the morning tourists idle at Nico's and Aldo's and the Cucciolo. Waiters hurry with cappuccinos or Coca-Cola, a flick of the wrist straightening the recently vacated chairs, lire gathered from beside empty cups and glasses. '*Prego, signori,*' newcomers are welcomed.

Prodding the ribs of Christ, St Thomas casts doubts in the Gallerie dell'Accademia, his wrist gently restrained while a cagey bishop awaits the outcome. From the arms of Bellini's Virgin her infant eyes the passing visitors, mouth open, plump. Beneath an orange tree Cima's version of the same has the Madonna grasping a livelier offspring, intent on wandering. Giorgione's storm breaks. St Ursula and her thousand virgins set sail on their great escape.

By the Accademia bridge an old woman feeds the cats, and in the park behind the Via Garibaldi another old woman feeds other cats, and in the Campo Manin the cats are fed by no one. The package tours file round the cathedral and hear the history of the Doges' Palace, then take time off, window-shopping in the Mercerie. On the Lido the gender academics argue in an air-conditioned conference facility. In the Calle Lunga San Barnaba a baker, Signor Colossi, makes ginger horsemen for the feast of San Martino.

It is cool in the *fondamente* that escape the sun, as it is in the Church of San Zaccaria and in the Church of the Frari and the Church of Santi Giovanni e Paolo, in Santa Maria Formosa and Santa

Maria della Salute. But on the Riva degli Schiavoni the autumn visitors
catch what they imagine may be the last of the season's warmth. There
are fewer of them than there were a week ago, and next week there will
be fewer still. In a fortnight there'll be beds to spare in the Danieli and
the Saturnia and the Londra Palace; the little Do Pozzi and the flowery
Gabrielli Sandwirth will close their doors, and the waiter at the Pensione
Bucintoro will return to his farm in the Alps when the ceremony of the
Votive Bridge has taken place. In December, with great to-do, there'll
be the hauling down of the flags in the Piazza San Marco.

A Strauss waltz plays at Florian's now, and at Quadri's there's Scott
Joplin. Mrs Haye is lost in a reverie of admiration, her bespectacled gaze
fixed on the green horses above the doorway of the basilica, only two of
them on view today, as often is the case. The great bell of the bell tower
is struck by its obedient *campanari*, who judder back to their hiding-place
as soon as their task is complete. 'Hi,' Mr Haye greets his wife, returning
at last with a film for his Olympus. '*Prego, signore?*' a waiter responds to
his summoning gesture.

The Czech national orchestra head for the basilica, their voices
low. '*Ecco, signore!*' the waiter announces, placing a glass of preprandial
gin and tonic, with nuts to nibble, in front of Mr Haye. 'Honey, you
should cut down,' his wife, from habit, rebukes. Two tables away an
English couple, with all the wondering freshness of a honeymoon pair,
smile shyly at one another. A kind of paradise this square is, the girl
whispers, and her husband of a day looks round to see if anyone has
heard. Mr Haye photographs a pigeon.

The trade of this city is in people now. Trade is what put it on the map;
trade is what keeps it there. Without its visitors, Venice would crumble
into dust, as the campanile of San Marco did in 1902. Since the time of
the Crusades, Venetians have made their fortune through dealings with
travellers, offering merchandise that has often been dubiously acquired.
No other Italians have intrigued as cleverly, bargained as keenly or
flattered their visitors as judiciously. The warlike Crusaders gave way
to the Holy Land pilgrims, whose stopover in Venice was softened by
Venetian hospitality at carefully calculated rates.

'Everything was done to make agreeable the period of waiting in
Venice for their ship to be made ready to sail,' writes Mr Links. A
predecessor in the guide-book business, Brother Fabri of Germany,
was held up for thirty-one days and occupied his time viewing the

remains of saints. For this purpose, writes Mr Links, he escorted his fellow pilgrims 'into at least one church a day, and often several. In the inevitable travel book which followed his return (they were almost as thick on the ground as they are today) he recounted how they had seen seventeen separate complete bodies, plus "many" Holy Innocents at Murano, and almost innumerable heads, arms, hands and fingers.'

Mr Links is a less exhausting companion. He dawdles the tourist about this cultural Disneyland, resting him from time to time for a cup of coffee or a *prosecco*, drawing his attention *en passant* to a Gothic doorway, or a shirt shop 'that carries out orders with remarkable speed'. The Calle Seconda de l'Ascensione, the Salizzada San Moisè, the Campo San Moisè: Mr Links gestures without pausing in his progress. 'The frightful façade of S. Moisè' is as Ruskin described it, 'one of the basest school of the Renaissance'. And while baseness is being considered, Mr Links suggests, the nearby façade of the modern Bauer Grünwald Hotel should not be overlooked.

In these safe hands you wend your way from the church of Santa Maria Zobenigo ('manifestation of insolent atheism', according to Ruskin) to the Palazzo Barbarigo, to the Campo dei Frari, to the noisy Campo San Bartolomeo. By the time you've finished — having learnt a great deal about Isabella Teotochi Albrizzi, and something about the 'patriotic crone' who deliberately misdirected Pépin's fleet into the treacherous flats, and noted the spot where Katharine Hepburn fell into the canal in *Midsummer Madness* — you begin to wonder about Mr Links himself.

He was the Queen's furrier, and you see him as plump, with glasses: linen-suited, panama-hatted, amused by almost everything that catches his idling eye. Or is he tall and lean, still linen-clad, with a slender walking-stick he hangs on the backs of café chairs? In Venice he has eaten outside on Christmas Day. In Venice he knows better than to wade through the squares with his shoes off, and rolled-up trouser-ends, during the floods. Such inelegance does not suit Mr Links; and he's familiar with the condition of the water. He's aware that you always see Venice as a tourist; that there is no other way you can, unless you are Venetian. There is a pale; and we, and he, are beyond it. But in his company we manage to stay close to its boundary.

Trudging back to the Europa e Regina Hotel, Mrs Haye has still never heard of Mr Links. The honeymoon couple, bewildered with delight while the orchestra plays 'Always', share a green Michelin. But in a string bag, on the boat to Torcello, half hidden by *A is for Alibi* by Sue Grafton, is *Venice for Pleasure* by J.G. Links.

> From Burano to Torcello is only five minutes by boat and on arrival we are greeted by offers to take us down the tiny canal by gondola. We naturally walk and in ten minutes or less are at the unpretentious but luxurious Locanda Cipriani. Just past it is the Piazza and there we can see all there is to be seen in Torcello, which is a marble chair, two little palaces, the church of Santa Fosca — and the cathedral.

In the Campo dei Mori the guide surfaces again, open in the hands of a young man who reads it as he makes his way in the direction of the church of the Madonna dell' Orto: he's after Cima da Conegliano's *John the Baptist*. Ruskin brought his wife here, but the poor woman took fright at the Tintorettos, and Mr Links is sympathetic. Because hurrying from the church, Mrs Ruskin missed the Cima.

At midday the autumn tourists crowd the bar near the cathedral that is famous for shell-fish sandwiches and other lunchtime tit-bits (its *supplì* the best in Venice). Everything is taken in the hand, a tissue wrapping the rice-balls, a glass of icy Soave. The strawberry ice-cream tastes as good as when the fruit was fresh.

The doors of the churches have closed, except for those of the basilica: the tranquillity of afternoon descends. Postcards are written, the sense of wonderment and carnival conveyed to less extraordinary places. In the Hotel La Fenice et des Artistes a couple make noisy love, their bed-head clattering against their neighbours' wall. Mrs Haye snoozes in the Europa e Regina. Signor Colossi watches afternoon television in the Calle Lunga San Barnaba.

Life returns at teatime. The Venetians lead out their muzzled dogs. With fresh vigour an aria from *Così fan Tutte* is tried again, the sound floating down from an upstairs window. San Donato and San Marziale unbolt their doors. Smoking a cigar, a man in a hurry strides purposefully to the altar of San Giorgio dei Greci as if to assault it, but only aims his view-finder. Lire drop into ecclesiastical coin-boxes, illuminating saints and angels and holy infants all over again.

The air is mellow now, and already the *passerelle* are in place — metal trestles that support planks to walk on — a few feet above the level of the anticipated floods. Workmen hurry over the refurbishing of boats in the Stazioni Marittime; the first creosote has been applied to the rafts of the Zattere. Grey spreads into the sky; yesterday's evening warmth does not arrive. Long before dusk the first of the season's fogs is hardly more than a mist on the Giudecca. Wisps of it creep eerily through the Arsenal. Gum boots are pushed to the fore in less fashionable shoe-shops.

Their conference on the Lido over, the gender people have reached the Piazza San Marco, half-heartedly intent on a night out. They come from all academic disciplines and from many countries. Gender is their common language: how it governs all human circumstances, all pictures ever painted, all sculpture, all literature, all thought; or equally how it does not. On the Lido they have aired their theories and their passionate views; there have been anger and disdain and just occasionally agreement. In the Piazza San Marco their exchanges continue.

Scattered over the tables in the square, they do not quite relax: they see no reason to. Fierce in their certainties, the historians correct history; field-workers peddle gender problems from the Andes and the Himalayas. Literary theorists recite the conclusions of their theses; sociologists explode another myth. Of both sexes themselves, young and old, the gender experts speak of Foucault and Henke and Jessica Benjamin, and discourse on phallocentric voices. The music of the orchestras is faintly registered as an irritant. If Mr Links went by they wouldn't notice.

All around them the less abstracted have a jollier time. German heads wag over German beer, toes tap to 'Edelweiss'. The French make plans for tomorrow, the English write more postcards. The Dutch are there in force, with the Japanese and the Australians, Belgians, Swiss, Swedes, Danes, Spaniards, Americans, an Indian prince, an Irish priest. The aperitif hour is when strangers fall in love and *far niente* is what matters most, when the Venetians insist that being a tourist is fun, and tips are generous.

The Czech national orchestra depart. They've had a good day. They've seen the Bridge of Sighs and been told all about it. They've seen the Ca' d'Oro, glass being blown, and the ceiling of the Senate Chamber. Entranced, they've crowded round the windows that display a suitcase, a wash-bag, trousers and flimsy underwear: all carved in wood.

Refreshed by her doze, Mrs Haye from Wisconsin points a policeman

194

out to her husband: he takes another photograph. In the cake-shops the ginger horsemen that honour St Martin are more in evidence than they were yesterday, some decorated with icing, some simpler. Signor Colossi's are the best.

The lights flicker on in the arcades, in the shop windows, on the ornamental lamp-posts. '*San Martino! Pan e vino!*' children chant, playing in the Campo Santa Margherita. The Ponte del Ravano is sketched in the dusk, and near the Zattere a statuette of St Agnes. The noisy after-hours chatter in the Campo San Luca lessens as the office-workers drift home. The waiters finish eating in the Da Ivo and the Antica Carbonera and the good-value restaurant of the Calle della Madonna. The dinner trade begins.

An hour later, the fog is real, sweeping in from the lagoon. On the Riva it swirls about the landing stages, blurring the rosy lamplight. With candles flickering in a gondola, a Japanese business party slides down a dark canal. Elsewhere a coffin is conveyed. When night falls, *calle* and *fondamenta* are silent. Then footsteps echo and fade, a voice for a moment chatters on the boothless telephone of a *campo*. In the fog, Venice is more of a marvel than ever.

In autumn, winter, summer or spring, in sun, rain or snow, no one can do justice to this city: Mr Links would be the first to agree. No guidebook can convey a fraction of its unique character, any more than the hard-working art guides can add to the splendour of Carpaccio or Bastiani by picking over the details of their canvases.

Florence has the best of Donatello and Fra Angelico, Cimabue and Giotto and Ghirlandaio. Rome has its Forum and its Pope, Bologna its arcades, Pisa its tower. Genoa has its recipes, Milan its style, Siena its *Palio*, Fano its beautiful women and a Perugino Annunciation. Montepulciano is the most felicitous of all the Tuscan hill towns. Pienza is a jewel. San Gimignano does you good just to be there, Monticchiello takes your breath away, Sansepolcro has Piero della Francesca's masterpiece. In Italy, in city after city and town after town, you can go on for ever. But compound all there is and the remarkable presence of Venice would still not be surpassed.

From its rickety beginnings — logs jammed into the sticky mud of the lagoon — it struck a defiant note that is still there as it precariously survives. The mainland Italians who had sought refuge on the islands of the lagoon from the barbarian hordes in the fifth century were a medley

of fishermen and traders whom few observers guessed would ever pool their interests. But they did, astutely realising that such observers — from Genoa in particular — were ready to move in on them, and remembering that it was for safety's sake they had settled where they were. They knew about the sea, they knew about mud; they learnt what they had to learn about the piles upon which they were to build their headquarters. *La Serenissima* they dubbed it, but in spite of that grandiose title practicalities came first: elegance followed when there was time for it. In their combining one with the other the Venetians developed the genius that, plan by plan, stone by stone, created their wonder of the world. It took deviousness and determination, and patience and perception, the acquiring of new skills, the harnessing of greed, but eventually it was there.

Night closes most of it down on this particular November day and when dawn lightens the sky, by some lucky chance the fog has slipped away. The bell towers of Santi Apostoli and San Giovanni Elemosinario, the spires of San Polo and San Barnaba, emerge from a cool morning twilight. The first hand-carts clatter over the Ponte del Ravano and the Ponte Santa Maria Formosa. Stacked with the day's first vegetables, the motor-boats chug to the markets. The daytime *vaporetti* join the all-night service of Line One.

Tourists leave, new tourists arrive. The out-of-season academics fly away, to argue elsewhere on the conference trail. A group of travel agents flies in, brightly labelled with name-tags that advertise the tour operator at whose expense they are being offered a sight of the goods they sell. The members of Reigate and Crawley Art Cities Club step refreshed from their overnight train, ready for their bargain outing in November. This morning is much the same in Venice as yesterday morning was, including a fact that wise Mr Links is careful to warn about: someone today also will find the whole dazzling enterprise too much of a good thing.

(1992)

The Nire

COUNTY TIPPERARY IS divided into two: the North Riding and the South Riding. The town of Clonmel — Cluain Meala, the honey meadow — is the administrative centre of the South Riding, and the capital of the county. It's interesting in all sorts of ways: a town of the ancient territory of the Decies, Anglo-Norman, massively fortified in the fourteenth century — a protection that stood it in good stead when Cromwell, riding by, decided to besiege it.

The River Suir gives Clonmel much of its character, and the mountains that surround it add something to that, but the town has its own provincial idiosyncrasy. Spacious O'Connell Street, Gladstone Street and Irishtown may be a far cry from a honey meadow, but the centuries that have passed since this was a designation have left an insistent mark. There is a faded grandeur about Clonmel: a prosperous past is evoked by the Georgian symmetry of Anne Street, by the mill buildings of the Quakers, the mementoes of Carlo Bianconi, the Main Guard. The West Gate, with a plaque to a native — Laurence Sterne — was rebuilt in the 1830s. Greater antiquity is mostly buried, or remains in bits and pieces. Somewhere beneath Old St Mary's church are the foundations of the Church of Our Ladye of Clonmel, built when the de Burgo family was the one that locally mattered most. The Abbey of St Francis has a fourteenth-century tower.

You begin in Clonmel when you walk out of the realities of the twentieth century into the timeless stretches of the Nire Valley. Personally, I begin at Hickey's bakery with a cup of coffee in Nuala's tiny coffee shop, then drive south into County Waterford. Bungalows with handkerchief trees and fancy façades decorate the roadside, each one vying with the next. At Ballymacarbry there's Doocey's filling station and grocery. At Melody's lounge bar you turn off and head for the hills.

Between the Monavullagh Mountains and the Comeraghs, the River

Nire — or Nier — descends from Coumalocha and is repeatedly joined by tributaries of its own en route to becoming a tributary of the Suir, west of Newcastle. The ascent to Coumalocha begins ordinarily enough, and so do you if you choose the lane through Lyre, leaving behind you when you begin your walk a couple of old vans that serve as sheep shelters, the ruins of a house usefully adapted as a docking pen, and two scarecrows that are the hillside's protection for its lambs. The going is easy until the bogs begin, the incline gentle. You walk in a balm of silence, hardly disturbed by the larks that dart out of the bracken or become agitated above your head if their nests seem endangered by the tramp of your feet. After heavy rain the areas of bog pose a problem; you do your best to skirt them.

The scarecrows have lost their outlines when you look back. The vans are coloured dots. The farmhouse, the red barn roof, the clump of firs, are nothing much either. The ground is drier after an hour or so, the ascent steeper. Seefin, Coumfea, Milk Hill, Knockaunapeebra, Crotty's Rock: slowly you move into their territory, welcomed only by sheep. But there are foxes here too, their holes among the rocks. And buzzards hang stealthily.

When you reach the first of the corrie lakes, tucked in below Coumfea, the silence seems almost palpable. The dark water is as still as ice, and as cold. The lake has a lonely look up there on its own, as if aware that it has been forgotten. Steeply encasing it, the mountain of which it's a part rises on three sides; looking up, you can guess where the first of the higher lakes is — similarly cradled, similarly fed by an orderly torrent that disappears when it goes underground.

I met an old man once in the Nire Valley. He was poking his way along the lane at Lyre. He said he had walked to Waterford in his youth, thirty miles away. He said he had walked to Cork, which is more than sixty. He didn't like roads, he never had. I asked him why he'd walked to Waterford and Cork, and he explained that he had wanted to see them. The time he was talking about was 1910 or so, he couldn't be certain exactly. But whenever it was, he insisted, in those days people walked more in Ireland. There was a man he knew who walked from Waterford to Dublin.

The encounter was unusual because you don't meet many people when you leave the beaten track in the Nire Valley. Usually you meet no one at all. But occasionally a dog is barking, miles away, scurrying after the sheep. On distant roads, cars creep along the Nire Drive; busy on a slope, a tractor goes about its task as leisurely as a snail.

There are other places as peaceful, but outside Ireland there are few in Europe as accessible. For the imaginative walker, the temptation is to find the Nire's bleak splendour a symbol for the island that contains it, as in the past other elements have been symbols of the Irish whole. James Clarence Mangan's 'seas of corn' were that. Kilcash was that, and the Tipperary Woodlands, and St Columba's little oak grove. Patrick Kavanagh saw it in the black hills of Shancoduff, Yeats in his lake isle.

But, somehow, in the Nire poetry is limited, there being no human connection, nor a past to mourn. No Mass was ever said here, no earls arrayed themselves in splendour, no different landscape can be regretted. Yet looking down from these modest heights at lush fields and managed forests, you feel that here, not there, the elusive spirit of Ireland might just possibly be — not packaged as Dark Rosaleen or Cathleen ní Houlihan or the Old Woman of Beare, but in the chilly air and sheep scratching for nourishment. Nature is defiant on Europe's western rock, and you would swear that this Ireland all around you has never been different. It is the only wisp of romance you are offered as you tramp on, up to the next small lake.

It's a personal attachment, of course: your own place. For others, there is Kerry or Connemara, the Wicklow Hills, Donegal, Mayo; and it is rarely easy to assess why fondness for particular landscape comes about. All you know is that affectionately you remember where the patches of cropped grass are, the ferns, the gulches, the best approach when the going's mushy, the way around the shale. It is affection, you are equally aware, that causes you to want to know what you never will: every single yard of this vast place intimately, in all weathers, at every time of day. The secret of beauty may be here, and probably is, but it isn't yours to discover either. All there is, as you descend, is a litany of sounds that echoes perfectly what you see: Knockanaffrin, Knockeen, Spilloge Loughs, Shanballyanne, Fauscoum, Glenahiry, Toorala.

In Hickey's bakery, where yesterday's bread is still being sold at reduced prices, the spell cast by that landscape doesn't evaporate. It seems irrelevant that a man has reached a hundred and two in Thomastown, as the *Nationalist* reports, or that there's been malicious damage at the Rock of Cashel. In Nuala's coffee shop housewives consume barm brack and tea, an elderly couple decide on salad sandwiches, young mothers quieten their children with cake. The talk is of the Strawberry Fair, and the Clonmel Festival Majorettes on parade. The town has had its first new heart, and next week will have a new mayor. The *Nationalist* reports that a Clonmel man has been warned that wives are not footballs to be kicked around; three publicans have been fined for after-hours offences; Tipp's last hope of a title is the minor hurlers on Sunday. In Hickey's bakery the real world presses its claims again, ephemeral, mortal.

(1992)